# FORGIVING OTHERS, FORGIVING OURSELVES

## Understanding & Healing Our Emotional Wounds

Myra Warren Isenhart, PhD & Michael Spangle, PhD

*Walking Together, Finding the Way®*

SKYLIGHT PATHS®
PUBLISHING

Woodstock, Vermont

*Forgiving Others, Forgiving Ourselves:*
*Understanding and Healing Our Emotional Wounds*

2015 Quality Paperback Edition, First Printing
© 2015 by Myra Warren Isenhart and Michael Spangle

For information regarding permission to reprint material from this book, please write or fax your request to SkyLight Paths Publishing, Permissions Department, at the address / fax number listed below, or email your request to permissions@skylightpaths.com.

**Library of Congress Cataloging-in-Publication Data**
Isenhart, Myra Warren, 1936–
Forgiving others, forgiving ourselves : understanding and healing our emotional wounds / Myra Warren Isenhart, PhD & Michael Spangle, PhD.
     pages cm
Includes bibliographical references.
   ISBN 978-1-59473-600-1 (pbk.) — ISBN 978-1-59473-610-0 (ebook)  1.  Forgiveness.
2. Emotions. I. Spangle, Michael. II. Title.
BF637.F67I84 2015
155.9'2—dc23
                                        2015018374

10  9  8  7  6  5  4  3  2  1
Manufactured in the United States of America
Cover Design: Jenny Buono
Cover art: © agsandrew / Shutterstock
Interior Design: Michael J. Myers

*Walking Together, Finding the Way*
Published by SkyLight Paths Publishing
A Division of LongHill Partners, Inc.
Sunset Farm Offices, Route 4, P.O. Box 237
Woodstock, VT 05091
Tel: (802) 457-4000 Fax: (802) 457-4004
www.skylightpaths.com

This book is dedicated to the students, teachers, colleagues, friends, and family members who helped me reach the vantage point needed to see this topic clearly.

To my students, especially David and Rob,

To my teachers, especially Miss Wittmeier and Dr. Dance,

To my colleagues, especially Gary and Tom,
To my friends, especially Phyllis, Charles, and Liz,
And especially to my husband, Frank, who
belayed me every step of the way.
—Myra Warren Isenhart

Dedicated to the wonderful university students who have blessed my life through the years. May you know how much I cherish what you have taught me and how you've blessed me with your friendship.
—Michael Spangle

# CONTENTS

# INTRODUCTION ──────────

After her husband's affair, a wife mourns the loss of her marriage. A saddened father grieves over the death of his teenage son, who was killed by a fellow student at school. A woman speaks of her profound sadness after learning that her pastor had committed indiscretions in his role at the church. The pastor, burdened with guilt, yearns to be welcomed back by his worship community. An adult son grapples with his anger toward his emotionally abusive father. An employee tries to work through her resentment toward her boss after she is passed over for an important promotion.

Each of these incidents left the victim with emotional wounds, looking for healing and a way to let go of devastating memories. In any of these examples, extending forgiveness is not easy. Instead, it is a journey that requires patience and effort. A desire to inflict comparable pain or to see justice served may halt progress. For some people, forgiveness may require an apology from the transgressor. Others may need to see the offender behaving in a way that shows a change of heart before they can forgive. In this book, we will explore many ways people journey toward forgiveness.

Aside from serious harms that permanently affect our lives, small events also call for forgiveness. These include getting over an annoying comment made by a family member, forgiving a close friend who disappoints you, or letting go of anger toward a work colleague who made a remark that embarrassed you in a meeting.

We believe that seeking and granting forgiveness is foundational in nearly all relationships. Forgiveness demonstrates our willingness to learn from our mistakes and become the kind of person our relationships demand. Forgiveness provides a bridge over sadness, disappointment, and failure. If you don't cross that bridge, you can carry emotional burdens for years— even decades. When you don't allow others to cross that bridge, you close the door on meaningful relationships. You may even prolong the suffering of those seeking forgiveness, including people you know and love.

It is typically easier to forgive other people than it is to forgive yourself. Sometimes adults describe still feeling guilty years later about lying to a parent, stealing as a teenager, or letting down someone important in their lives. Because they can't change their past actions, many people carry these disappointments through their entire lives. This book will show you that self-forgiveness may involve probing your motivations and asking uncomfortable questions about your own self-concept. Avoiding this work can damage personal development; accepting it may free you to live a fuller, more honest and honorable life.

This book also addresses how you can help people around you in their efforts to seek or grant forgiveness. This is especially important for counselors, pastors, mediators, coworkers, or even members of your own family. We offer you strategies and tactics for helping people in your life let go of longtime burdens that have caused them emotional pain. Helping others give or receive forgiveness enables us to be peacemakers in our world.

## Your Partners on the Journey

The core of this book is drawn from our experience as longtime practitioners of forgiveness in many settings. We have more than twenty-five years of experience in conflict management, helping disputing parties such as families, churches, businesses, schools, hospitals, and even between the leaders of major churches work through problems. Inability to forgive was at the core of many of these disputes. In our work we serve as mediators both individually and jointly, helping people begin their journeys toward forgiveness.

To support our work, we conducted a study to learn more about how people deal with forgiveness. In this study, 278 participants completed written surveys and had an opportunity to describe a time in their lives when they experienced forgiveness. The participants ranged in age from twenty to eighty, and education levels spanned high school graduates through those with advanced degrees. About two-thirds of the participants were females. We were amazed to discover that people from a wide range of religious backgrounds, ages, and levels of education had similar views on forgiveness.

Throughout this book you will find stories from people we've worked with over the years, including those who took part in our survey. To protect their anonymity, we have not used their real names. In some cases the stories are composites based on more than one person's experience. Some grammatical revisions have been made to original wording supplied by survey respondents.

## A Note on the Spiritual Content

While we as authors draw from our Christian background, the voices you will encounter throughout this book are from a variety of spiritual and religious traditions, primarily the Abrahamic faiths (Judaism, Christianity, and Islam), or no religion at all. In an effort to make this book accessible to a broad audience, we vary the terms describing the spiritual energy within us, from God as characterized in the Abrahamic religious traditions to concepts such as Divine, Spirit, Higher Power, or Inner Light. While we do draw examples from the Abrahamic faiths as we explore forgiveness, this book is not intended to be an in-depth examination of forgiveness views and practices of any one faith. In delving into the spiritual level of forgiveness, we seek to identify the role of forgiveness as it relates to the energy, meaning, and purpose that infuse our personalities with life, rather than how it relates to organized religion.

## Our Approach to Forgiveness

Forgiveness involves three dimensions: forgiving others, being forgiven by others, and forgiving yourself. While these may seem like three different actions, we see no distinction with regard to the definition of forgiveness. Forgiveness is the process of letting go, whether it is canceling a debt, granting pardon for a wrong committed, or releasing emotions related to being harmed. Just as the word *love* encompasses giving love, receiving love, or loving ourselves, the forgiveness process follows the same dynamics. If I have committed a wrong against someone and I apologize, I am asking her for grace and the willingness to cancel my emotional debt. If someone commits a wrong against me, I must decide whether I am willing to extend grace to him and let go of the emotional pain I feel.

So throughout this book, we use the word *forgiveness* in a similar comprehensive manner. The purpose of the book is to help readers build skills in three areas:

1. Asking someone for forgiveness
2. Granting forgiveness when it's requested by another person
3. Forgiving yourself for past actions or thoughts

The word *forgiveness* is appropriate in all three settings.

In our professional work as well as in our personal lives, we have both witnessed the power of forgiveness as well as the devastating sense of loss that comes from withholding forgiveness. We invite you to journey with us as we explore all the dimensions of forgiveness, learning how to apply this gift to yourself and your life, as well as using it to guide others toward a happier, more peaceful existence.

# CHAPTER 1

# THE NATURE OF FORGIVENESS

## BEGIN WITH A CLEAR UNDERSTANDING

> Our task is not to fix the blame for the past,
> but to fix the course for the future.
>
> —John F. Kennedy

Forgiveness is fundamental to our emotional health and our ability to create healthy relationships. When you make mistakes and say things you regret, forgiveness can repair what is broken, sometimes within you and at other times between you and others. Unfortunately, most people harbor misconceptions about forgiveness. For example, forgiveness does not necessarily mean reconciliation with someone who has done you harm. It does not mean that there is no longer a need for an apology or assurances that the harm will not occur again. And while you may be willing to forgive others, self-forgiveness may be the hardest task of all.

In this chapter, we explore what forgiveness is and what it is not. We clarify what we mean when we say *forgiveness*, as well as exploring the many perspectives on this complex emotional response.

## The Meaning of Forgiveness

Granting true forgiveness involves giving up anger, bitterness, or resentment toward an offender and releasing pent-up negative energy. For some people, this means suspending a long-standing grudge or giving up thoughts of revenge. When the offender is a friend or family member, forgiveness may require letting go of negative feelings that have festered for years.

1

Stanford psychologist Fred Luskin characterizes granting forgiveness as the feeling of peace that emerges when you take a hurt less personally and choose to limit or end your suffering.[1] Expressing a similar view, meditation instructor Jack Kornfield describes how granting forgiveness releases the past's grip on your heart, freeing you to live more fully in the present.[2]

In the case of minor offenses, such as when a spouse forgets an anniversary or a friend fails to follow through on a commitment, forgiveness may come quickly and easily. A conscious decision to pardon the offender may be all that is required in these situations. But for more serious offenses, such as infidelity or betrayal, the path to forgiveness may take many years. Psychologist Everett Worthington posits that granting forgiveness takes a change of heart in which sympathy or compassion replaces anger, bitterness, or feelings of revenge.[3] Sometimes forgiveness involves changing how you think about another person.

You can also view forgiveness from the perspective of healing. For example, when you have been harmed by someone, you might experience a loss of innocence, self-confidence, your perception of safety, your value to others, or love. Emotionally, forgiveness enables you to push the RESET button and reduce the power of the negative emotions affecting your life. Psychologically, forgiveness can free you from negative thinking that preoccupies your mind. From a spiritual point of view, forgiveness enables you to allow God to heal your emotional wounds.

> Forgiveness is the fragrance the violet sheds on the heel that has crushed it.
>
> —Mark Twain

Many people have trouble with the word *forgiveness*, sometimes so much that it blocks their ability to move past the harm done to them. For these people, it might work better to describe forgiveness as the process of *letting go*. This phrase allows a person to achieve the same outcome without stumbling over the word *forgive*. Letting go releases negative emotions and the power of the past over the present.

Carl grew up in a small town in the Midwest. To the outside world, everything about his home life appeared normal—he had a steady job, a loving wife, and a welcoming home. But for most of his growing-up years, Carl was bullied and abused by his father, and this pain left Carl with festering emotional wounds. Over and over in his mind, he heard his father's brutal words, "You are my bastard child. You were conceived before I married your mother. So in the eyes of God, you are worth nothing."

As the years went by, Carl's relationship with his father became more volatile. During high school, Carl endured both physical and emotional abuse at the hands of his father. The day after he graduated from high school, he left home and moved to another state.

Every few years, Carl returned home to visit his brothers, to whom Carl's father showed more grace and kindness, but Carl rarely spoke to his father. He showed his disdain by sleeping in a camper, rather than in his father's home. In return, his father refused to place Carl's wedding photo on the wall with the other family pictures. The absence of Carl's picture in the family photo gallery served as a constant reminder that he was not loved or valued by his father.

But when Carl reached his sixties, he made a decision. He said, "That's enough. I'm going to let go of the past and I'm going to forgive my father." Although his father was now elderly and in failing health, Carl started making overtures to renew the relationship he had lost.

On one of his trips, he brought his wife, Ann, who was also trying to heal the relationship. During this visit, Ann worked hard at being kind to her father-in-law. When he complained about his aching feet, Ann knelt on the floor in front of him and massaged them. Suddenly, Carl's father looked up at her and said, "There's something missing. We need to have your wedding photo on the wall with my other sons." Within minutes, someone brought out one of Carl's wedding pictures and hung it in the family gallery with the other photos. As the picture went up, Carl hugged his father. In that moment, the display of that single photo symbolized acceptance by Carl's father and Carl was able to forgive him.

## What Forgiveness Is Not

Most pastors and psychologists agree that genuine forgiveness goes beyond simply "forgiving and forgetting." You don't need to repress or condone painful experiences to move toward forgiveness. In fact, the old adage "forgive and forget" may do more harm than good. Recent neuroscience research conducted by University of St. Andrews researchers suggests that forgetting rarely promotes forgiveness. However, in many cases, forgiveness may promote forgetting.[4] In other words, if you want to get over something, forgiveness is a good start.

Forgiveness does not mean condoning harmful actions, forgetting painful experiences, or justifying bad behavior. But, in some cases, reflecting on harmful experiences can offer insights into people and situations. For example, recalling details of a harmful experience may show you how to avoid being victimized again. Or perhaps steering clear of people who make you feel vulnerable can prevent you from falling into harmful patterns. This was true for John, who had a rocky relationship with his mother.

> Every time I went home, I came back with severe anxiety, created by my mother's criticism. She didn't like my job, the person I married, or the other life choices I'd made. When I chose to forgive her for her behavior, I began to reflect on how disappointed she was with her own choices in life and how she was taking it out on me. Once I got that, I changed my thinking about her and about her critical comments. Our relationship improved and so did my anxiety level when I went to visit her.

Of course, true forgiveness does not mean excusing bad behavior. No one has a right to harm you. When you choose to forgive, you do not give up the right to feel that an offense was unfair. At the same time, you are not required to give the offender a get-out-of-jail-free card for actions that have harmed you. Pope Benedict XVI maintained that forgiveness does not replace a need for justice.[5] There is a clear distinction between forgiveness and amnesty, which grants a general pardon without requiring offenders to repent, apologize, or compensate for wrongs committed. Even though you may choose to forgive someone, you can still require her to face the consequences of harming you. These consequences might include something as drastic as a prison term, financial restitution, or even accepting the end of a personal or professional relationship.

> As long as you don't forgive, who and whatever it is will occupy a rent-free space in your mind.
>
> —ISABELLE HOLLAND

Embracing forgiveness does not mean allowing yourself to be hurt without reaction. The Jesuit writers Dennis, Sheila, and Matthew Linn make the point in *Don't Forgive Too Soon* that "turning the other cheek" does not mean acceding to poor treatment by others.[6] The authors give many examples of how this may be done. Our favorite involves the rabbi who discovered that his synagogue had been defaced by graffiti, including swastikas. The police identified a group of male college students who admitted responsibility. Before the judge could sentence them, the rabbi intervened to ask that they be released to study Judaism with him. In this way, the young men were spared a police record and developed an appreciation for the Jewish faith. We see this as a creative solution that both rejects the harm and rehabilitates those who committed it.

In addition, repetitive harm does not call for repetitive forgiveness. When a friend, colleague, or loved one continues to harm you, despite understanding your feelings, forgiveness may not be what the situation requires. Instead, you may need to negotiate an agreement about boundaries in the relationship and be willing to enforce whatever consequences are associated

> Forgiveness is like faith. You have to keep reviving it.
>
> —MASON COOLEY

with crossing those boundaries. If this does not work, you may have to decide whether to leave the relationship or to stay because of the relationship's value to you. For example, a woman who is physically or emotionally abused by her husband may forgive him, but she might also choose to leave the marriage if he does not agree to stop the abusive behavior. A woman may feel verbally demeaned each time she visits her parents' home. She can explain that if they continue this behavior, she may still love them and even forgive them, but to protect herself she will limit her interaction with them to occasional phone calls.

When you grant forgiveness, that does not give people permission to continually invade your emotional boundaries. Rather, forgiveness frees you from the power someone might appear to have over you. You can say two things simultaneously: "I forgive you, because it is good for me, but, at the same time, I will not allow you to harm me again."

Mary's father repeatedly criticized her approach to raising her children. Her children's problem behavior was particularly likely to occur at holiday gatherings in front of extended family and guests. For example, when Mary's youngest child refused to eat any vegetables, it confirmed her father's belief that her parenting style was entirely too permissive.

This situation is not about forgiveness as much as redefining relationship issues. Assuming she has previously raised this issue with her father, Mary has several options. She can leave the table when he criticizes her. She might agree to come to holiday dinners only if he stops being so critical. Or she may even decide that the family relationships are too valuable to make a fuss and choose to ignore him. This last approach is not forgiveness; it is simply choosing to "live with it."

**Who are we to judge?**

**—POPE FRANCIS**

In our experience, authentic forgiveness cannot be required, meaning one person cannot demand it from another. For example, as children, many of us were told by adults, "Say you're sorry." This can lead to a superficial apology, in which we say, "I'm sorry" because it is expected, not because it is true. While that parental practice may be justified in the name of instilling good habits, it does not necessarily lead to an authentic process of forgiveness.

When you've endured serious harm, you need to consider the level of pain caused by the offense, the value of the relationship, and whether the act was intentional or not. You may struggle with these issues for days, months, even years before you are ready to move toward forgiveness. You cannot will yourself to "just do it" and expect to wake up the next morning relieved of your anger or resentment. Forgiveness requires patience as well as time for healing.

## Questions

1. Based on your experiences, how would you define *forgiveness*?

2. Describe times when you have had difficulty letting go of negative feelings associated with particular experiences. What made letting go difficult?

3. If someone has wronged you, what do you require of the wrongdoer in order for you to release bad feelings you may harbor?

# CHAPTER 2

# WAYS WE EXPERIENCE FORGIVENESS

## THREE PERSPECTIVES ON HARM WITHIN AND BETWEEN US

> To forgive is to set a prisoner free and
> discover that the prisoner was you.
>
> —Lewis Smedes

People express their forgiveness of others in many ways. How a person who has been harmed chooses to respond depends on many factors, including who committed the harm, the seriousness of the harm, and the type of relationship she has with the transgressor. Among the more common types of responses are the following:

**Grace.** This response involves unconditional compassion and mercy. Because the wounded person has great resilience, patience, and capacity for self-repair, he is able to dismiss the harm and continue the relationship without anger or resentment.

**Working through emotions.** In this response, the person forgives as her negative emotions subside. This allows her to let go of the harm done without placing demands on the transgressor.

**Dialogue.** In this response, the person forgives the offender after talking through the issue with him. The victim wants to learn why the deed was committed and how the transgressor feels about what was done. Through conversation, healing begins and negative emotions fade away.

**Conditional.** In this response the wounded person essentially says, "I will forgive you if ..." Once the transgressor agrees to the specified conditions, the wounded person may want a promise and assurance that the act will not be committed again.

Forgiveness also occurs across three different dimensions: you may need to forgive someone, you might need to be forgiven by someone, or you might need to forgive yourself. You can experience forgiveness in one of the dimensions and not another. Or the timing may be different for experiencing each of the dimensions. For example, you could forgive your friend today but take months or longer to forgive yourself.

Nancy grew up in a home where her mother managed conflict by screaming at anyone who got in her way. Whenever she realized that her mother was angry, Nancy hid under the bedcovers and cried. When she was a teenager, Nancy chose to show love to her mother and forgive her for those violent outbursts. But she also concluded that her mother's outbursts were her fault because she hadn't been the kind of daughter her mother wanted her to be. Her inability to forgive herself contributed to years of poor self-esteem and lack of self-confidence.

As an adult, Nancy went through a transformation that helped her understand how miserable her mother's life had been. She began to see that her mother's anger was less about her and more about her mother's life. With this new understanding, Nancy slowly let go of her self-critical thinking and her belief that she needed to always please her mother. Eventually, she gave herself the gift of forgiveness, the same gift she had given her mother years ago. Nancy's change of heart demonstrates that sometimes forgiveness means trying to view an offending person apart from the offense.

Although forgiveness can't erase the memories of past harm, it can heal painful emotions associated with those memories. When you forgive someone, you pardon that person and lift the grudge that you harbor. You can also choose to pardon yourself, just as you granted forgiveness to others. Even if a relationship is not repaired, you can still feel released from the negative emotions associated with that relationship.

# Three Perspectives on Forgiveness

We have found in our research that three perspectives on forgiveness can help foster emotional repair:

> *Psychological forgiveness* confers freedom from distressing thoughts or unwanted emotions for both the offender and the wounded person.
>
> *Relational forgiveness* refers to suspending harmful communication or behavior and engaging in efforts to repair the relationship, such as by offering or accepting an apology or other words that demonstrate the offender's understanding of the harm committed.
>
> *Spiritual forgiveness* relates to healing the spirit within us. Pursuing spiritual forgiveness calls for finding meaning and receiving pardon from sources understood as Sacred or God, and regaining a sense of inner peace and harmony.

## *The Psychological Perspective on Forgiveness: Restoring the Self*

When you approach forgiveness from a psychological perspective, you may be trying to forgive yourself for something you've done, looking to understand why something bothers you so much, or seeking freedom from unwelcome thoughts. While other perspectives focus on restoring relationships or healing your spirit, the psychological perspective on forgiveness focuses primarily on the benefit of forgiveness for restoring the self.

When you believe someone has treated you unfairly, you may feel a range of emotions, such as anger, disappointment, sadness, or betrayal. Offensive words and actions can foster doubt within you, bruise your self-esteem, or undermine your self-confidence. Damage to your self-concept can last for months or, in many cases, years.

Psychological harm gives rise to self-doubt. You might ask yourself, "What's wrong with me that would make someone want to harm me?"

Sometimes grief and anger promote myriad conflicting emotions that never seem to go away. Every time you see the person who harmed you, the feelings well up again. In the psychological perspective, forgiveness requires you to overcome the emotional triggers within you.

While the psychological perspective helps you look at why you took an offense so personally, it may also help to consider the source of your resentment. You may need to ask yourself, "What's the real issue here? What made this event cause me such distress? Could I sit down and talk about it with the person who harmed me?" Sometimes, using this perspective, you can explore ways to heal the thinking that crystallized in disappointment or distrust. Consider asking yourself, "Why does this bother me?" As you look at your history of forgiving, you might also discover why you are vulnerable to certain kinds of offenses more than others.

> To forgive is the highest and most beautiful form of love. In return, you will receive peace and happiness.
>
> —ROBERT MULLER

### *The Relational Perspective on Forgiveness: Repairing the Bridge Between Us*

When someone disappoints you, breaks an agreement, or violates your trust, the relationship can be severely harmed. Lack of respect, insensitive behavior, and betrayal might all characterize relational damage. While the psychological perspective describes what goes on *within* us, the relational perspective focuses on what goes on *between* us.

For example, Sam and his brother, Robert, were competitive growing up. But the competition boiled over when Robert asked Sam's girlfriend to the high school prom. The girl said yes and eventually she and Robert got married. Sam felt betrayed by both his brother and his girlfriend, and he vowed never to speak to his brother again. At age eighty, Sam could still recount the details of that event as though it were yesterday. He said, "I kept my promise. I've never spoken to my brother again." His emotional hurt ran so deep that it caused him to give up a relationship with his brother for a lifetime.

Forgiving typically involves letting go of feelings about the past. But Sam had something going on inside him that he couldn't let go of. If he had recognized this truth, it would have required a psychological shift for him to let go of the feelings of betrayal he had maintained for a lifetime. To repair this relationship, Sam believed his brother needed to offer a genuine apology or demonstrate repentant behavior.

You count on your closest relationships, such as those with family members, to make your life safe and predictable, and to be harbors of trust. So when these relationships fail you, forgiveness is difficult. Your fear, anger, and sadness may escalate to a point where they shut down your conversations. Until these emotions subside, forgiveness may not be possible. Once you have cooled down, you may need to process the event that triggered your anger or frustration. Before sharing your thoughts with others, consider answering questions like these:

- What need of mine didn't get met?
- What set me off?
- What do I need from this person to get over my pain?

Being clear about your needs will help those who've harmed you understand your feelings and hopefully encourage them to offer forgiveness. You also have to be patient and give others a second chance to rebuild the relationship.

To achieve forgiveness in your important relationships often requires both grace and compassion. When forgiveness is supported by grace—unconditional mercy—it gives you both a second chance and the ability to make things right. A second and related factor that enhances forgiveness is compassion. Laura Davis, a leading voice on reconciliation, defines compassion as "the ability to see another clearly, without illusion, from a place of loving kindness. Compassion enables you to try to understand why someone hurt you and at the same time care about their hurt."[1] Compassion takes courage because, even as you extend

> Forgiveness does not change the past, but it does enlarge the future.
>
> —PAUL BOESE

compassion to others, you are never quite sure how they will respond. Buddhist teacher Pema Chödrön suggests that "compassion practice is daring. It involves learning to relax and allow ourselves to move gently toward what scares us."[2] Compassion encompasses grace because you admit that you yourself have made mistakes and recognize that others have as well.

Without compassion, apologies may be perceived as cold and insincere, and the words *I'm sorry* may appear manipulative. Spiritual leader and peace activist Thich Nhat Hanh explains, "Only when compassion is born in your heart is it possible to forgive."[3] Compassion demonstrated in words of genuine concern, by the offender or offended, enhances the possibility of healing and trust. Psychologist Robert Enright combines grace and compassion with his assessment that in many situations forgiveness involves the practice of gentleness and a softened heart, in spite of what others have done.[4]

To explain forgiveness from a relational perspective, we use the concept of "relational identity." In a marriage, we might ask the wounded person, "What does this wrongdoing mean for you as a couple?" We then look at how each of the parties now defines the relationship and what each one's expectations are. For example, following an extramarital affair, George commented, "We're still married but I would describe our life together more as coexistence than I would as a happily married couple."

In the relational perspective, we attempt to repair damage to relationships. Someone takes the risk of saying, "We can get past this." Then forgiveness serves as a bridge to rebuilding trust, promoting heartfelt communication or restoring confidence in the relationship. But in many cases, relational forgiveness doesn't come easily.

Rebecca and her mother, Ellen, had always maintained a close and loving relationship. But as Rebecca got older, she began to resent her mother's frequent criticism of her choice of friends as well as male partners. One Sunday at a family gathering, as Ellen began her typical tirade about her daughter's life choices, Rebecca snapped. She exploded at her mom and the conversation escalated until they were both shouting.

Suddenly, Rebecca grabbed her coat and left the house. From that point on, she and her mother stopped speaking to each other. In this close-knit family, the loss of this loving relationship affected everyone. Planning for holidays or family events became agonizing because Rebecca and her mom refused to be in the same room with each other.

Eventually, Rebecca moved away and later married and had children. Over the years, Rebecca's aunt Janet stayed in touch with both Rebecca and Ellen, showing love and acceptance while sharing details about each of their lives with the other. But Rebecca and her mom continued their rift and refused to communicate or offer forgiveness.

Decades after that fateful quarrel, Ellen was diagnosed with terminal cancer. Hoping this would create a way for mother and daughter to reconcile,

Aunt Janet immediately called Rebecca and begged her to come home. Rebecca, however, did not relent. She refused to visit her dying mother, and did not even attend her mother's funeral.

Three years later Rebecca was also diagnosed with cancer. At that point, she called her aunt Janet and asked for help in making amends. With the guidance of her loving aunt, Rebecca let go of her anger and bitterness. As she underwent the successful treatment of her own cancer, Rebecca made a clear decision to forgive her mother for that fateful argument as well as the other times when her mom had been critical or judgmental. She said, "I want to remember my mother the way she was during the years of our warm and loving relationship. So I'm letting go of all the rest."

Oftentimes, relational forgiveness requires you to accept others or the dynamics of a relationship as less than perfect. Forgiving may call for a great deal of patience, compassion for the problems and challenges in other people's lives, and communication that values the other.

## *The Spiritual Perspective on Forgiveness: Surrendering to That Which Is Beyond Us*

While the psychological perspective on forgiveness primarily deals with healing the self and the relational perspective focuses on healing a relationship, the spiritual perspective values both of these. Forgiveness at this level may involve establishing or deepening a relationship with God or developing greater awareness of what your spirit needs. When you're disappointed with the way life has gone or with your own failures, looking outside yourself for spiritual support can be a source of comfort, strength, and direction. Sometimes you may feel disconnected from people or even disconnected from yourself. You may even sense that you've failed yourself or the Spirit that created you and that you need a divine source to cleanse your spirit. This dimension of forgiveness has to do with getting things right *within* yourself.

> Forgiveness is a virtue of the brave.
>
> —INDIRA GANDHI

Achieving forgiveness through a deep relationship with God has been demonstrated for us time and again by African American churches in the United States. We have witnessed forgiveness demonstrated by black and white congregants following such disasters as the 1963 16th Street

Baptist Church bombing in Birmingham, Alabama, that killed four young girls. We saw it again in the late 1960s, 1970s, and 1980s when die-hard segregationists burned a number of churches across the south. In 2015, a white supremacist at the weeknight prayer service of the Emanuel AME (African Methodist Episcopal) Church in Charleston, South Carolina, shot and killed nine African American people, including the pastor. This historic church was most likely targeted because of its leadership role in racial matters, including speeches by Rev. Martin Luther King Jr. during the civil rights era. Despite repeated attacks of violence, black church institutions, so vital to southern blacks since days of slavery, have found spiritual healing and eventually forgiveness.

"We come together as a reminder that God loves us and that we are forgiven."[5] This was the opening remark by Pastor Norvel Goff as he preached at the first service after the tragedy at Emanuel AME. It was clear from his following remarks that forgiveness is embodied in the spirituality of this Christian tradition. In his view, sometimes we cannot understand or surmount challenges, or we confront evil in the world, or there are losses beyond our control and complications we cannot comprehend. We give these over to God or whatever we name the Divine Spirit that unites us all. The scripture offered by Pastor Goff was Psalm 46, "God is our refuge and our hope." Black churches are grounded in the theology of love.

> He who cannot forgive breaks the bridge over which he himself must pass.
>
> —CONFUCIUS

The spirituality of individuals who lost loved ones in this senseless shooting must have been sorely tested. However, at the bond hearing of the jailed shooter, families of some of the victims told the perpetrator of their forgiveness. As one said, "I forgive you but I don't want to be around at Judgment Day when you are called."[6] President Barack Obama called the forgiveness of those relatives "an expression of faith that is unimaginable but that reflects the goodness of the American people."[7] Many of us outside the black churches may wonder or even doubt if we have the spiritual resources to achieve such a level of forgiveness. Whether or not any individual can, it is an inspirational goal for all.

In the Christian Scriptures, the Greek word *aphiemi* is used for forgiveness. The word literally means "to release" or "to let go," including letting go of past harm that still burdens you. Christian traditions teach that we are to forgive because we have been forgiven by God. A Jewish view holds that in order to be forgiven, a person must first admit to wrongful action and repent. Islam has two important terms for forgiveness: *afw*, which means "pardon" or "amnesty," and *tasamuh*, which means "tolerance." The two words are used interchangeably to convey a forgiving attitude.

A news report described an event that demonstrated the power of Islamic forgiveness.[8] The story begins in 2007 during a street fight in Iran near the Caspian Sea, when a nineteen-year-old man named Balal killed the seventeen-year-old son of Maryam Hosseinzadeh. A court found Balal guilty of the crime and ordered him to be hanged. As the time came for the hanging and Balal stood in the gallows, his mother sat weeping on the grass, convinced that she would lose her son. In preparation for the hanging, an executioner blindfolded Balal. Suddenly, in an extraordinary move, Maryam stepped forward and instead of kicking the chair out from under Balal to cause his death, she slapped him on the cheek and yelled, "Forgiven!" Maryam and her husband then took the blindfold off the young man and he was freed. According to Islamic law, Balal was guilty and deserved punishment. But in this case, the people who had been harmed held both the capacity to forgive and the ability to free him from his transgression. Later, after he stepped down from the gallows, Balal described the slap as "the space between revenge and forgiveness."

Sometimes, talking about forgiveness from the spiritual perspective is difficult because spirit overlaps with elements normally associated with the psychological perspective. However, emotions can affect the strength and vitality of the spirit and a broken spirit can influence how someone thinks and feels. The two are closely related.

Forgiveness seeks to promote redemptive remembering, which means remembering the past but with grace and understanding. Oftentimes, this means forgiving ourselves for being vulnerable as well as promoting greater acceptance of others who may have failed us. In *Forgiveness Considered*, Father Henry Charles explains:

> The freedom the victim secures through this process is larger than
> the freedom from hostility, negative feelings, and remembered

pain. It is a freedom to reconstruct one's life from a richer tapestry of experience.[9]

## When All Three Perspectives Occur in a Relationship

Don grew up in a blended family with children from several marriages by both of his parents. To manage the blend, his father became a tyrant, eventually throwing Don out of the house at age fifteen.

To achieve forgiveness, Don first had to deal with psychological issues, such as anger toward his father and guilt for not being the son his father wanted. Eventually, his inner struggle and disappointment shifted to focus on the relationship. As an adult, he was unsure how to relate to his father after years of abuse. His forgiveness involved seeing past the harsh way he had been treated, and trying to be pleasant whenever he saw his father.

By the end of his father's life, Don's forgiveness gained a spiritual dimension. After many years of bitterness, he decided it was time to give his father's behavior and his own resentment over to God. A few years before his father's death, Don reconciled with his father and experienced a deep level of healing.

As illustrated in Don's story, we have identified all three of the primary perspectives from which people approach forgiveness: psychological, relational, and spiritual. In some cases, we might experience all three at the same time, or we may begin in one domain and end in another, as Don did over the course of fifty years.

We experience the need to forgive or be forgiven in many different ways. For some, forgiveness may appear as a spiritual yearning for peace. For others, psychological self-doubt, anger, and, at times, even resentment may precede the drive to offer or accept forgiveness. And some experience deteriorating communication in an important relationship. If you are trying to get past a harm you have done or one that has been done to you, you need to focus on the perspective that matches your need. For spiritual issues—when you are searching for meaning in life experiences and inner peace—you need to work on resolving forgiveness issues with the Sacred. If the issue is psychological, you have to explore your inner sources of worry

> As far as the East is from the West, so far has he removed our transgressions from us.
>
> —PSALM 103:12

and anger. This may include considering the issue of self-forgiveness. And for those who have damage in relationships, the path may call for initiating a discussion with a friend or family member to resolve old wounds. For each of the perspectives, we must do different kinds of work if forgiveness is to be achieved.

In the chapters that follow, we explore ways to find peace through forgiveness in each of the different perspectives. We provide tactics for self-healing as well as the healing of broken relationships. And because we live in community, we conclude this journey with direction on how you can help those around you experience freedom through forgiveness. Let's begin the journey on this healing path together.

## Questions

1. How do you typically respond to situations requiring forgiveness: with grace, by working through your emotions, by encouraging dialogue, or by setting down conditions?

2. List some examples of the psychological, relational, and spiritual perspectives of forgiveness in your life?

3. What helps you get over harm that's been done to you?

# BENEFITS OF FORGIVING AND BEING FORGIVEN

## RELEASING THE PAST, EMBRACING THE FUTURE

> When you forgive, you in no way change the
> past, but you sure do change the future.
>
> —Bernard Meltzer

Forgiveness can have a positive impact on your thoughts, your emotions, your physical health, and your circle of friends. By contrast, holding onto disappointment, anger, regret, or guilt affects your physical health, your moods, and your relationships with others in negative ways. When you hold a grudge, others know about it. Forgiveness offers a gift of peace that can help you relax, calm your emotions, and improve your health.

## Avoiding the Emotional Drain

Nikki "ratted" on her friend's social behavior at work and is unable to forgive herself for doing so:

> I can never forgive myself for talking about my friend's social behavior at work. The word got around to management and she did not receive the promotion she expected. I'll never know how much difference that made, but when I confessed, she was certain it mattered. She claims to have forgiven me, but I cannot forgive myself.

19

So what? Why does forgiveness matter? In this case, Nikki is preoccupied by the event, she has low energy, and she is having trouble sleeping through the night because she worries about the consequences of her indiscretion. She is sad about the loss of the friendship and troubled by self-blame. She is even coming to view herself as someone who is incapable of keeping secrets or all too capable of injuring others.

Psychologist Robert Enright reports that what Nikki is experiencing is not uncommon when the path to forgiveness seems blocked.[1] When you cannot forgive others or yourself, you experience a loss of emotional energy and inattention to other matters because your focus is stuck on the past. Your emotional energy is spent managing anger and replaying the event in your mind. When you are aware that so much of your emotional energy is being diverted to events of the past, you may even become angry for not letting go. When it comes to self-forgiveness, the anger is compounded. The injured friend's offer of forgiveness did not automatically result in the Nikki's ability to forgive herself. Whether injuries are inflicted by yourself or others, the inability to forgive can bring your spirits down.

> Anger affects the levels of adrenaline in your body and this in turn affects every organ. Anger can make you ill.
>
> —ROBERT ENRIGHT

## Improving Your Physical Health through Forgiveness

Such distress is not limited to your mind. Negative feelings have a tendency to set off a relentless, self-reinforcing cycle of deleterious consequences for both mind and body. When anger is new, your heart beats faster, blood rushes to your internal organs, and your pulse speeds up. Your body is primed for fight or flight. Those reactions may immediately follow a serious offense. Other symptoms include blushing, a queasy stomach, or feeling faint. If you were victimized a long time ago and still vividly recall the event, those feelings can make you feel depressed. Whatever the case, whatever the degree of awareness, your body experiences the sense of being harmed.

Medical researchers find that when we are able to forgive others for harming us, there are measurable, positive physiological effects for cardiovascular disease and back pain.[2] For instance, heart attack patients demonstrated less anger and hostility when they behaved in a forgiving way; those negative emotions are associated with cardiovascular risk. Even more impressive, the forgiving group had lower rates of death. Other medical research demonstrates that the ability to forgive is associated with lower blood pressure. Psychotherapists working with clients to achieve forgiveness find similar beneficial physiological outcomes.

Back pain is one of the most common reasons that patients see their internists. While there are multiple causes for this malady, medical researchers find a link to forgiveness for many sufferers. The book *Anger Kills: Seventeen Strategies for Controlling the Hostility That Can Harm Your Health* by Redford and Virginia Williams summarizes studies of people with chronic back pain; those who were able to forgive others had lower levels of pain and fewer medical problems, such as anger and depression, than the unforgiving subjects. The same studies found that resentment toward the offender is likely to aggravate back pain. The connection between back pain and forgiveness runs in both directions: back pain tends to worsen for those who hold grudges, while those who are capable of forgiveness experience pain relief.[3]

## Preserving Family Ties through Forgiveness

Many of us have experienced situations in which a family member committed an act we cannot sanction. We may see our inability to forgive as a personal decision, but often there are broader implications. Garry, a young man in our survey, could not forgive his uncle and no longer speaks to him because of a decision the uncle made when it came to Garry's terminally ill grandmother: "I can never forgive my uncle for pulling the plug on my grandmother. She might have recovered from the stroke and did not deserve to die."

The rift between nephew and uncle means that the family, uncomfortable with having them both under the same roof, must leave one of them out of family gatherings. This creates a wider quarrel about which of them to invite to what events. The uncle and the nephew are eager to gather allies in this conflict, so other family members are subjected to their bad-mouthing one another and forced to take sides. The absence of forgiveness has cascading consequences for the entire family.

The transforming impact of forgiveness on one relationship—that between Garry and his uncle—can halt the damage within the family and restore or preserve relationships valuable to the offended person's life. For example, if Garry's mother takes the uncle's side in Garry's conflict with his uncle, her relationship with her other child could be interrupted for an extended period, causing long-term negative consequences. However, if the nephew and his uncle can work through their conflict and restore a meaningful relationship, the entire family will experience relief.

Finally, the invitation to forgive may appeal to parents who wish to model a more positive stance for their children. As John F. Kennedy said, "Let us not seek to fix the blame for the past. Let us accept our own responsibility for the future."[4]

## Tightening the Weave of Our Communities

Talia was an active member of her religious community. She reports that she was "crushed" by a breach of friendship within the group.

> The act I couldn't forgive was committed by a pastor's wife who had been a close friend. When I took over Women's Ministries in the church, I became very close to someone the pastor's wife didn't like. Over time, the pastor's wife came to avoid me completely and would leave the room any time I entered. She refused to speak to me.
>
> I had practically worshipped the ground she walked on and was crushed. For months, I never voiced my concerns or asked to resolve the issue. Finally, I asked if we could get together to talk about whatever had gone wrong. We met and she behaved badly—she didn't acknowledge the reason she behaved so distantly—and to this day I can only guess at the problem's roots.

If you have ever been active in a church, synagogue, or mosque, you will know that if the spiritual leader's wife leaves the room every time you enter, her actions would be noted, talked about, interpreted, and perhaps even acted upon by other members. Such behavior begins to unravel the fabric of even the tightest community.

Secular communities and workplaces also suffer when relationships among their members are fractured by a lack of forgiveness. These breaks result in loss of supportive relationships, disrupted communications, distraction from responsibilities, a decrease in productivity, and impaired reputations, among other undesirable outcomes. In their article "Managers as Negotiators," Carol Watson and L. Richard Hoffman report that more than 40 percent of management time is spent addressing unresolved conflicts.[5] If you work outside the home, you deal with coworkers more than you interact with family members. You see your close colleagues daily; you depend on healthy relationships with them to complete your work successfully. Inevitably you will need to forgive and be forgiven at work, regarding anything from insensitive comments to backstabbing.

Luella, a young woman in our survey, explains that she will never be able to forgive the manager who harassed her:

> I was sexually harassed and bullied by my supervisor, who is an openly lesbian woman. She ignored my requests to stop sending me notes and touching me when I walked by her desk. I was embarrassed, humiliated, and eventually asked for a transfer to avoid her behavior. I can never forgive her.

As you might expect, Luella's coworkers were aware of the situation. Some felt she was misinterpreting the manager's friendly behavior and overreacting. Others sided with Luella and encouraged her to report the manager to the Human Resources Department. All were distracted from their responsibilities, resulting in deadlines missed and clients poorly served. Both the individual and the group were suffering. Luella expressed a wish to work through forgiveness for herself on this issue but has no desire to reconcile with the manager or return to the group.

> We must let go of the life we planned, so as to have the life that is waiting for us.
>
> —E. M. FORSTER

Dr. Charles Griswold, a professor of philosophy at Harvard and Boston University, emphasizes the compelling need of communities for just relationships among the members. In his view, "Forgiveness is neither a therapeutic technique nor simply self-regarding in its motivation; it is fundamentally a moral relation between self and other."[6] The entire community benefits when moral relations between individuals are restored.

We find that the capacity for and tendency toward forgiveness is practiced not only within human communities but also by our primate ancestors. To be strong and survive, nonhuman primates have evolved ways to resolve conflicts among their members: they participate in peaceful postconflict reconciliations with their opponents. These peaceful contacts relieve the stress of conflict and allow the animal group to enjoy the benefits of living in community.

Frans de Waal, a noted anthropologist, has studied conciliatory behavior among primates for many years.[7] He finds that friendly behaviors, such as kissing, submissive sounds, touching, and embracing, are quite common after an altercation. In fact, these behaviors are more common subsequent to conflict than they are during peaceful periods. De Waal has primarily studied chimpanzees, but similar patterns have been found among the bonobo, long-tailed macaques, and mountain gorillas. Indeed, it turns out that goats, sheep, dolphins, and hyenas all tend to reconcile after conflicts. Researchers offer a similar rationale as that noted above: forgiveness and repair of relationships among individual members provide a survival advantage for the group.

> Anger can be a major complicating factor in the treatment of persistent pain.
>
> —J. W. CARSON

Do human communities have such natural capacities for giving and receiving forgiveness? Evolutionary science argues that we do. While tales of revenge sell more newspapers than stories of forgiveness, we can just as readily relate instances of forgiveness where it would seem impossible to achieve. Along with the capacity for revenge, the capacity for forgiveness offers an intrinsic evolutionary advantage for human communities. Science writer Michael McCullough reasons that because forgiveness helped ancestral humans survive as a community, it is now typical of modern humans.[8] While natural selection has caused forgiveness and reconciliation to be universal features of human nature, cultural differences and other phenomena influence the frequency with which it is practiced and how it is done.

## The Ripple Effect of Forgiveness

There are many reasons to seek forgiveness. Some relate to decreasing personal pain, both psychological and physiological. Any distress you feel will inevitably manifest in relationships with significant others. Another motive for seeking forgiveness is to mend fractured relationships among close friends and family. The ripple effect of unresolved conflict is also evident in sacred and secular communities, and within workplaces and houses of worship. The practice of forgiveness in organizations results in more transparent communication, a greater focus on the mission of the organization, and increased satisfaction for members and those they serve. At every level, there are compelling reasons to practice forgiveness.

## Questions

1. What physical feelings do you experience when someone does something to you that requires your forgiveness?

2. How have you been affected by someone else's quarrel?

3. How might your family benefit if you were to achieve forgiveness in a relationship important to you?

4. What are the needs for forgiveness in a community in which you are involved?

5. When has lack of forgiveness affected your workplace? How? Who were the players and what was the outcome?

# CHAPTER 4

# RESISTING THE PRACTICE OF FORGIVENESS

## WHY SUCH DIFFICULTIES?

> Who takes vengeance or bears a grudge acts like
> one who, having cut one hand while handling a knife,
> avenges himself by stabbing the other hand.
>
> —Jerusalem Talmud, Nedarim 9:4

Given all the benefits of forgiveness for individuals, relationships, and communities, why is the practice of forgiveness so difficult? Understanding resistance to forgiving others is critical to achieving the healing of forgiveness. Some resistance is rooted in our psychology, some is relationship-based, and some reflects the norms of forgiveness within certain communities.

## The Desire for Revenge Is Normal

Human nature combines both positive characteristics, like empathy, and negative characteristics, such as anger. Both kinds of traits occur in psychologically healthy humans. Ideally, a mature person expresses anger within a loving relationship in ways that keep the relationship intact. The ideal isn't always the case, however. In *The Forgiving Self*, psychologist Robert Karen writes, "A totally forgiving self is neither possible nor desirable. Hatred, revenge, and striving for justice ... are as much a part of us as love and the wish to make amends."[1]

Anthropologist Michael McCullough agrees that the desire for revenge is normal. In his article "The Forgiveness Instinct," he states, "It's normal in the sense that every neurologically intact human being on the planet has the biological hardware for it."[2] In this article, McCullough goes on to speculate about why revenge might have evolved in humans. First, revenge may have discouraged aggression from potential enemies. Our ancestors lived in small groups and conflicts were obvious to everyone in the community. If the targets of aggression didn't fight back, their passivity might have invited further aggression. Recent psychological experiments demonstrate this same dynamic. When others witness a conflict taking place, there is a greater likelihood that the person who is attacked will retaliate.

Another theory of revenge is that it may have been a way to deter an aggressor from attacking again. Living together in tight bands, our ancestors did not have the option of ending relationships. Leaving the group was not an option because working as a group was essential for survival. Exile was typically used as a punishment that was akin to death. Revenge discouraged bullies from initiating further conflicts.

Finally, revenge may have evolved as a way to promote cooperation. Living in hunter/gatherer bands, our ancestors could not tolerate individuals who acted selfishly. If individuals did not share food or they enjoyed the safety of the group without making a contribution, revenge directed against them established the importance of cooperation to survival.

## The Satisfaction of Playing the Victim

Another difficulty we have with forgiving others is that none of us reaches adulthood without wounds. Human nature guarantees that even the most loved and well-cared-for children will bring childhood disappointments into their adult relationships. Most of us are not aware of such wounds and avoid the pain of them by remaining unaware. The problem is that we unconsciously act out those flawed experiences in our significant adult relationships. When you bury feelings, you bury them alive.

While wounds may surface in many ways, one of the most common is the adoption of the victim role. For example, the child who lost a parent or whose parent was hostile or withdrawn sometimes finds solace in the role of martyr and uses that as an excuse to resist forgiving others. Jamie carries childhood trauma from her relationship with her mother:

I was a pain to my mom and I grew up knowing that. She never spent any money on me, so I grew up wearing secondhand and clearance clothes. As a result, I was severely ostracized as a child. My mother is also a recluse, so she didn't socialize and would never let me have friends over. Since I was ignored at school and she was alone, she became my only friend and encouraged my emotional dependence on her. But if I did something to offend her, she would "divorce" me and not talk to me for months. As a result, I have serious problems forming and retaining relationships.

Jamie has taken an important step toward self-understanding by acknowledging the link between her mother's behavior and her own relationship difficulties as an adult. Without reflection on or understanding of our insecurities, we become stuck in the repetition of childhood harm and don't recognize our need for forgiveness.

Others slip into the victim role without such awareness. For instance, as a child, Lois suffered from her parents' divorce and her mother's reputed preference for her brother. Now a senior citizen, Lois will recount those childhood wrongs whenever anyone will listen, complaining that she never had a birthday party, never got new clothes, and always had to vacuum the house while her mother worked. As an adult, she finds that few people appreciate her work or notice her achievements. Even fewer are to be trusted. Lois will not be able to forgive others until she understands how her childhood wounds color her adult patterns and works to forgive her mother.

Why would anyone continue to be so fixed on the past? There are certain satisfactions in the role of martyr, such as blaming others for whatever adult shortcomings we might have. "If only ..." relieves us of the need to take responsibility for our more recent actions or inactions, such as a failure to engage in the work of healing. It may garner sympathy from those who listen to our complaints. At a deeper level, it shields the victim from experiencing the pain of that childhood loss again. In Lois's case, by refusing to forgive her parents for her imperfect childhood, she has a ready-made excuse for anything that goes wrong in her life.

## The Comfort of Denial

Denial is another common ploy we use in resisting the urge to forgive others. In *Forgiveness: How to Make Peace with Your Past and Get On with Your*

*Life*, Sydney Simon and Suzanne Simon write, "Denial is as comfortable as old sneakers, as sticky as flypaper, as automatic as breathing, and habit forming to boot ... which is why we can get stuck in denial for a long, long time."[3] We reassure ourselves that a harm isn't worth confronting in spite of the hold it has over our thoughts and behavior. We tell ourselves, "It really isn't a big deal because everyone has issues to deal with." Or we say, "That was yesterday" in order to minimize our hurts. By downwardly revising the harm in our own minds, denial puts forgiveness out of conscious reach.

## Boundaries Around Our Willingness to Forgive Others

We make decisions about whether or not to forgive based on assessments of the offense and the offender. Whether consciously or unconsciously, we consider:

- The nature of the offense
- The motivation of the perpetrator
- The offender's acknowledgment of wrongdoing
- The offender's willingness to make amends

The more significant the offense, the more likely you will not forgive or will need more time to process it. In our survey, the offenses that were the most difficult or impossible to forgive tended to be quite serious, such as rape, undermining of a career, or an action that caused the death of a family member.

Clear patterns within primary relationships also emerge. In our survey, the most difficult offense to forgive was physical or emotional abuse by parents. Among friends, the hardest offense to forgive was a broken confidence. Within intimate relationships, infidelity and physical violence were frequently mentioned as difficult or impossible to forgive.

In the case where actions contribute to death, forgiveness can be especially difficult. Jim told us:

> When my cousin put her daughter in a tub full of scalding-hot water, causing severe burns, she did not seek medical attention for the child. Two days later, the daughter died. After burying her body, my cousin and her boyfriend went to the police and

reported that her daughter had been kidnapped. A few weeks later, they finally told the police what had happened and both she and her boyfriend were convicted of child abuse resulting in death.

In addition to the gruesome nature of this offense, the cousin hid the child's death and lied to authorities. According to Jim, his cousin's unwillingness to acknowledge harm or to make amends tilted the scale even further against his extending forgiveness.

This is not to argue that forgiveness is impossible when life-and-death issues are at stake. As we know, some people forgive others, even if they've committed a heinous crime. For example, the parents of twenty-six-year-old Stanford graduate student Amy Biehl, who was raped and murdered by a street gang in South Africa, forgave those who had taken their daughter's life. In addition, they have invested their time and resources in bettering the lives of street youth in Cape Town, South Africa. It appears that the seriousness of an offense is only one factor, albeit a critical one, in whether we forgive.

In our work we see that resistance to forgiveness varies not in exact correlation to the nature of the act but rather in how we interpret it, as illustrated by Maria's story:

> My uncle by marriage took me aside and told me what a horrible young woman I had become. He took me to a parking lot alone and belittled me and yelled at me, making me cry. He told me my parents had done a poor job raising me. That crossed the line. I realize he was using me to express his own anger and frustration. But at this time, I am still unable to forgive him.

Maria recognizes that her uncle was using her to express negative emotions. She made a judgment that unloading frustration on an innocent person "crossed the line." In this case, the line represents the boundary of her expectations about a particular behavior. In her mind, forgiveness for an offense on the other side of that boundary is not possible.

Tom Mauser is the father of Dan, one of the students slain in 2001 at Columbine High School, in Littleton, Colorado. In his book, *Walking in Daniel's Shoes*, Mauser describes his own movement toward forgiveness as "measured," noting that some acts are easier to forgive than others. He makes a distinction between ignorance and knowledge, feeling that it is much more difficult to forgive an act that is intentional, thoughtless, or hurtful. He also finds that forgiveness is more difficult when the offender seems to lack remorse for the harm caused.[4]

Quite a few of our survey participants pointed out that they could not forgive acts of cruelty, especially when directed at children. Sally's comment is an example:

> Acts that challenge my capacity to forgive are terrorism and harming innocent people for an ideology or a criminal purpose. The events of 9/11 are still vivid in my mind and I still struggle with forgiving those who were responsible. I find it difficult to forgive Nathan Dunlap, who murdered five innocent people at the Chuck E. Cheese restaurant in Aurora, Colorado. I don't dwell on these acts, but when they are mentioned, I still hope there is a special hell for the people who committed those acts.

In our survey, we found that our respondents regarded damage to the broader community as unforgivable. For Lorenzo, one of our survey participants, a moral judgment stood in the way of forgiveness: "In some cases, lies that hurt our community, both the financial and the quality of life, are difficult or impossible to forgive."

Lorenzo is making a judgment, disapproving of private gain at the expense of public good. He is also commenting on the lack of regret for harm to the community. This is not to argue that all actions deserve forgiveness, either immediately or after some effort toward forgiveness has been made. Each of us must generate our own moral standards and apply them to our own behavior and that of others. As we do, ethical judgments may become barriers to forgiveness.

## The Security of the Familiar

Anxiety about the future is a common source of resistance to forgiving others. To the extent that you can tolerate the offenses of others or have found ways to work around them, you may not want to open up your suffering to them. After all, you have experience with this pattern and you know what to expect, no matter how unpleasant that may be. Especially if the other person is more powerful than you are, why would you want to risk making things even worse for yourself? The old adage "Better to deal with the devil we know ..." undoubtedly contains some folk wisdom. Certainly, there are better and worse times to confront a wrongdoer, and circumstances that are more conducive to reflection than others. However, convincing yourself that an offense by a more powerful person "wasn't so bad" is another mechanism that puts forgiveness out of reach.

## Falling Short of Our Expectations

When those close to you fall short of your expectations, you may become more resistant to forgiving. For example, Lorena, a college student, had an especially difficult time with forgiveness because of the trusting nature of her relationship with her boyfriend:

> My boyfriend cheated on me. He kissed another girl and let her sleep in his bed. The violation that was hard to forgive was that he lied to me about it. I was date-raped in college and had a harder time forgiving my boyfriend than I did the man who raped me, because I *trusted* my boyfriend.

Lorena has an expectation that when you're in an intimate relationship you're supposed to be sexually exclusive, and she expects that such a relationship will be characterized by honest communication. Her choice now will be to find another boyfriend who meets her expectations, to pressure her boyfriend to change his behavior, or to adjust her standards to fit the behavior of her current boyfriend.

Sometimes we hold expectations for the behavior of others outside our primary relationship. Sarah recounts this experience:

> My friend became involved with a married man. When I challenged her on it, based on her insistence that she wanted to help her kids have good marriages, she turned on me and said she was my friend only because I loaned her money and invited her to parties, dinners, and the like. We tried to work it out, but I was unwilling to let it go and she was unwilling to discontinue the relationship.

In this case, Sarah had expectations about her friend's morality that were violated when the friend continued to sleep with a married man. Sarah seemed to believe that it was her role as a friend to point out her friend's weak moral judgment and, if anyone ever found out about it, the bad example it would set for her friend's children. Perhaps at some level she felt the friend chose to continue the affair over maintaining the friendship with her. Expectations like these can impede forgiveness both within and outside of relationships.

## Lack of Childhood Exposure to Forgiveness

Forgiveness relates to the experiences you had as a child. If forgiveness was modeled by your parents, as an adult you are more likely to forgive others and yourself. Research finds a substantial correlation between parental modeling and the ability of children to forgive as adults. In our research, we asked people how forgiveness was handled in their families of origin. In that study, over half the subjects came from families where forgiveness was practiced. Adults modeled it for children; many of these participants said their parents encouraged and reinforced the practice of forgiveness.

However, roughly a third of the people in the study seldom or never saw adults modeling forgiveness. These respondents described family members who held grudges or gave a "cold shoulder" to other family members. One offered the example of brothers who stopped speaking over a hutch they both wanted when their parents died. The brother who got possession of the furniture item was never forgiven by the one who lost out, and none of his children were allowed to speak to anyone in that family. The inability to forgive extended across at least two generations and left the brother's children without models for family tolerance.

> I imagine one reason people cling to their hate so stubbornly is because once the hate is gone they'll be forced to deal with their pain.
>
> —JAMES BALDWIN

Ten percent of our study participants were grouped in a mixed category, some representing families where one parent modeled and encouraged forgiveness and the other didn't. Mixed groups also included families where parents insisted that children practice forgiveness but did not model it themselves. Respondents who received these mixed messages write rather cynical comments about forgiveness, such as, "I was expected to apologize, especially to my parents" or they were told to "forgive and never speak about it again." Adults who had no models for forgiveness or who came from families where there were mixed messages will have more difficulties with the practice of forgiveness than those for whom it was modeled and reinforced.

## No Acknowledgment of Wrongdoing

You will find it difficult to forgive if the person who harmed you does not see his behavior as wrong or recognize how you have been hurt. For example, Chris, a participant in our survey, experienced repetitive hurtful behavior from a parent:

> I have discussed my upset regarding this issue many times with this parent, to no avail. He does not acknowledge the behavior or the pain it causes me. I do not expect to ever receive an apology of any sort, so how could I achieve forgiveness?

In Chris's mind, the parent's refusal to acknowledge the harm in a repeated behavior prevents him from forgiving and precludes any further family reconciliation. This is not to say that there can never be forgiveness without apology, but in this case an apology would constitute acknowledgment. Short of this, forgiveness is not possible for Chris.

Many aspects of relationships may become barriers to forgiveness. Psychologist Robert Karen articulates what we know intuitively: "In the best of relationships there are islands of resentment that expand and contract with circumstances. Acceptance and rejection swim in and out of and around each other in complex ways."[5] Significant relationships will always include acts that require forgiveness; our hope is that none of these barriers proves insurmountable if you intend to preserve a relationship.

## The Influence of Community Norms

A variety of personal and interpersonal factors can be barriers to forgiving others. The influence of community norms on forgiveness is less apparent but just as powerful. We are aware that state and national governments have laws regarding the punishment of offenses but we forget that these developments are relatively recent—dating from about 5,500 years ago—in terms of human history.

Before the development of the modern state, the typical method of resolving major disputes was either through violence or payment of compensation, the choice to be determined by the offended individual. "An eye for an eye, a tooth for a tooth" was instituted to stop an offended person from imposing a more violent form of retribution than he had endured, thereby setting a community standard for violence. Indeed, anthropologist Jared Diamond reminds us there are contemporary societies where norms demanding revenge are still very much intact: urban gangs in America, Somalia, Afghanistan, the New Guinea Highlands, and countries where state control is weak but tribal ties are strong.[6]

In the New Guinea Highlands, each killing calls for a revenge killing. Most of the killings are caused by disputes over pigs or women. Villagers learn from early childhood to hate their enemies, to learn to fight, and to remember past harms that require revenge. Warriors who return to the village boasting of their kills and death on the battlefield are regarded as the most heroic. Offenses are resented by all members of the clan, who live and farm together. The personal responsibility for revenge killing technically falls on the victim's firstborn son, but if that child is too young, nephews or other clan members in the prime of life are expected to exact revenge. In societies like this, lacking strong state control, community norms not only create barriers to forgiving others but also consider forgiveness valueless.

> In my years as a pastor and teacher, I have found this obligation [forgiveness] to be the singular command of Jesus that ordinary Christians find most difficult to obey.
>
> —Fr. Henry Charles

For most of us, community norms do not resemble those of the New Guinea Highlands. We expect that appropriate punishment will be meted out by agencies of the state; it will not be our personal responsibility to exact revenge or determine the amount of restitution. If our home is robbed, we call the police. When the World Trade Center was attacked on 9/11, a commission decided on the amount of money to be paid to each victim's family. Of course, neither restitution nor legal judgment ensures forgiveness. We refrain from acting on personal feelings of revenge because we count on the state to deliver suitable judgments and punishments. For at least five hundred years since the time of Francis Bacon, we as a society have agreed with Bacon's view: "Revenge is a kind of wild justice, which the more man's nature runs to, the more ought law to weed it out."[7]

However, wartime experiences shed some light on how quickly our norms can approach those of the New Guinea Highlanders. Australian professor William Tidwell explains that national sentiment can dehumanize an enemy, a psychological process by which differences between our group identity and that of the enemy are exaggerated.[8] For instance, in World War II, the United States and its allies referred to both Germans and Japanese as lower forms of life, such as rats, vermin, scum, and pigs. In that instance, U.S. soldiers fought violently and brutally, some in hand-to-hand combat, to defend the United States and its allies. In most cases, the soldiers were welcomed home as heroes. Our need for security influences our judgments about who are—and who are not—worthy of forgiveness.

> We regularly ignore the fact that the thirst for vengeance is among the strongest of human emotions. Modern state societies permit and encourage us to express our love, anger, grief and fear, but not our thirst for vengeance.
>
> —JARED DIAMOND

In the 1960s during the war in Vietnam, community norms about revenge were in flux and dehumanization of the enemy was harder to maintain in an era when television covered the war zone. Seeing the faces of the enemy makes it harder to demonize them; therefore, those who killed them seemed less heroic. Returning veterans from this unpopular war were not widely celebrated and many suffered from post-traumatic stress disorder (PTSD). Norms relating to forgiveness and revenge may change dramatically, based on challenges to personal and national security.

Community norms relative to our willingness to forgive vary not only according to stressful circumstances but also within national boundaries. Violent practices erupt in modern times—revenge trumps forgiveness. The persistent desires to fly the Confederate flag and to begin community events with the singing of "Dixie" suggest that memories of the Civil War and resentment of that loss have not completely faded away in parts of the South. The brutal killing of Matthew Shepherd, the gay teenager who was tortured and left to die on a barbed-wire fence in Wyoming, is thought by some to represent Old West "justice," misapplied by drunken, homophobic youth. The media coverage of groups such as ISIS beheading Western journalists harkens back to harsh justice of earlier desert tribes. To some extent, past norms live on in present behavior.

Resistance to forgiveness may be linked to theology and historical wrongs. In the book *The Sunflower: On the Possibilities and Limits of Forgiveness*, Jewish Austrian Holocaust survivor Simon Wiesenthal, then imprisoned in a German concentration camp, tells a story about reaching the limits of forgiveness.[9] Brought out to work on the hospital's grounds one day, he was approached by a nurse who asked him to confirm that he was Jewish. When he did so, she told him to follow her. She led him to a room where a German SS officer lay dying of his wounds. The German told the prisoner that, following orders, he was guilty of burning a building with Jewish families inside. Now that he was dying, he repented for the deed, and he asked the prisoner, as a Jew, to forgive him. Wiesenthal struggled with the request, torn between compassion and justice, and eventually could not grant the dying man's request.

> In the beginning, we create the enemy. Before the weapon comes the image. We think others to death and then invent the battle axe or the ballistic missiles with which to actually kill them.
>
> —SAM KEEN

The rest of the book consists of essays by fifty-three distinguished writers offering their opinions about whether we have the right to forgive sins that are committed against others. Religious leaders, philosophers, and other serious thinkers do not reach consensus on this question. Indeed, most of the Jewish writers in the book believe that it is neither necessary nor possible in this instance, while most of the Christian writers called for compassion and forgiveness. Given the history of the Holocaust, the attempted genocide of the Jewish people, these differences are not surprising.

In the twenty-first century, a controversy over the new Canadian Museum for Human Rights also illustrates the barriers that cultural and national histories put in the way of forgiveness. Originally scheduled to open in 2014, the $351 million building has been repeatedly delayed by conflicts with groups that view their historical injuries differently than the curators do.[10] For instance, indigenous groups are furious that the museum does not plan to use the term *genocide* regarding their subjugation by British and French colonists. B'nai B'rith has protested the decision to exclude the founding of Israel from materials documenting the Holocaust.

Ukrainian-Canadians feel strongly that the 1932 famine-genocide perpetrated by the Soviet Union on Ukrainians (three million lives lost) should have its own gallery. The Canadian effort to identify and support human rights has clashed with memories that members of various groups feel must be honored. National pride and honor insist on cherishing historical wrongs and create barriers to forgiveness.

To the extent that community norms encourage revenge, forgiveness is inhibited. Where communities cling to past wrongs, where outside groups are dehumanized, and where violent behavior against traditional enemies is promoted, forgiveness is unlikely. Older, less civilized approaches to resolving conflict vary with geography and with periods of insecurity. In communities that lack rituals to enhance forgiveness and leaders to model it, forgiveness is uncommon. Forgiveness may be acted out individually, within interpersonal relationships, but it will be either encouraged or discouraged by the norms of the community within which the offense occurs.

## Questions

1. Why is it sometimes more difficult to forgive a loved one than someone who isn't as close to you?

2. Can you remember a time when you experienced a desire to avenge a hurtful act? Did you take revenge? Why or why not? If you did, was revenge satisfying?

3. When, if ever, is forgiveness possible without an apology?

4. What are the norms relating to forgiveness in your community?

5. How do you feel about offering forgiveness to someone who has harmed others?

CHAPTER 5

# WHAT FACILITATES FORGIVENESS?

## PERSONALITY, RELATIONSHIPS, AND COMMUNITIES

> The weak can never forgive. Forgiveness
> is the attribute of the strong.
>
> —Mahatma Gandhi

We all know there are many reasons that forgiving others may be difficult or impossible. However, some people achieve it and many others hold out the hope that it will happen in the future. What makes granting forgiveness possible? What is the basis for continued hope?

The journey to forgiveness is eased by a variety of factors. Particular personal attributes make forgiving behavior more likely to occur. Certain life experiences related to family modeling and religious belief often predispose us to practicing forgiveness. And, just as social norms can encourage us to seek revenge, community values that support conciliatory behaviors promote forgiveness.

## A Healthy Personality Aids the Willingness to Forgive

For the past few decades, researchers have been looking into personality traits that might be linked to a willingness to seek or grant forgiveness. It appears that people who practice forgiveness tend to have agreeable personalities and be focused on the future. Typically, they are healthy, both physically and emotionally. In general, people reluctant to seek or grant

41

forgiveness are likely to be past-oriented, lack openness, and demonstrate more self-punishing thinking. An additional factor involves sensitivity to circumstances. People who possess greater sensitivity to how and why an event occurred tend to be more forgiving than those who are less sensitive in this regard. Overall, forgiveness is more likely to occur among those who score higher on tests of psychological and physical health as well as those who are future-oriented and sensitive to circumstances.[1]

## The Important Role of Religion

Religious orientation also tends to be linked to a greater willingness to forgive. In our study, the overwhelming majority of participants endorsed the centrality of forgiveness to their religious traditions, which mainly included the Christian, Jewish, and Muslim faiths. For example, during the Jewish High Holy Days, Judaism has the Days of Repentance, ten days each year focused on repentance and forgiveness, reflection, and renewal. Many Christians observe Lent, a time of fasting, repentance, and reflection on Jesus's sacrifice and his teachings. Observant Muslims mark Lailat ul Bar, the Night of Forgiveness, by seeking forgiveness for their sins and believe that on this night a person's destiny is fixed for the year ahead. Based on these rituals and more, many of our survey participants reported that religion taught that forgiveness was "valued," "essential," or "central to their faith." Survey respondents explained that in worship communities, they learned it was important to say "I'm sorry" and to "forgive and forget." This finding is consistent with those of earlier researchers who noted a strong connection between religious upbringing, spiritual values, and the ability to forgive.

A few subjects in our study responded that they were not religious, and a small number did not know whether forgiveness was significant in their religion. A very small number claimed that forgiveness was not important to their tradition. If the results of past studies are valid, the unreligious and "don't knows" constitute a group who may have more difficulty with the practice of forgiveness.[2]

## Grace and the Unexpected Experience of Forgiveness

In some cases, you may experience changes in your psychological state that are very difficult to explain or account for; we refer to these as acts of grace. Our survey participants noted a number of ways they were able to release a grudge, including through reading and prayer. In our presentations, we have frequently heard from people who said they had long been frustrated by their inability to "get past" a significant hurt. Then suddenly, one morning they woke up to find that they had gotten past it completely. This occurred without further effort or explanation.

If you watched any of the horrific TV coverage of the Columbine High School shooting in 1999, you may recall the image of an injured teenager falling out of a school window. That teen was Patrick Ireland, who was shot twice in the head as well as in his feet. Rushed to a hospital, Patrick was in a coma for many days while his parents kept a bedside vigil. His first words upon awakening were, "Forgive them. Please forgive them." When his mother asked why, he replied, "Because they didn't know what they were doing."[3] Neither his own serious injuries nor the loss of dear friends prevented Patrick from instantly forgiving the shooters and encouraging others to do the same. Patrick's extension of forgiveness is an act of grace.

> We learn wisdom from failure much more than from success. And probably he who never made a mistake, never made a discovery.
>
> —SAMUEL SMILES

Psychotherapist Robert Karen writes, "Sometimes love comes on like a sudden liberating breeze ... some fundamental emotional tone is so altered that we feel like a different person, more endearing to ourselves and more tolerant of others."[4] Not every intrapersonal factor that facilitates forgiveness can be measured. The concept of grace from the spiritual model of forgiveness is one of those immeasurables.

## Age, Education, Gender—Do They Matter?

In addition to psychological conditions, researchers into forgiveness have investigated the relationship of demographic variables, such as age, education, and gender. While the results are not consistent, it is useful to recognize what variables *don't* make a difference in forgiveness. It is also fascinating to look at a few findings that are promising.

Age is not a reliable guide to a person's ability to forgive. Some researchers report that the propensity to forgive increases from adolescence to old age. Other studies have found no relationship, and our own recent research discovered that the inclination to forgive *decreased* with age. Given mixed and contrary results, we cannot rely on age as a predictor of the willingness to forgive.[5]

If age isn't an indicator, what about education? Again, results vary. Some studies found differences among educational levels—those whose education only went through secondary school were less forgiving than university graduates. Many studies show no significant correlation between the level of a person's educational achievement and her propensity for seeking or granting forgiveness. Our own study revealed that the higher the educational level, the less likely people were to forgive. More definitive research is needed.

Gender differences are no more consistent with regard to forgiveness than are age or education. Some researchers found women to be more forgiving than men. Others reported no difference between men and women but found a significant difference in the likelihood to forgive among parents with multiple children. It appeared that the more children they had, the more forgiving the parents were.[6]

In our own study, we found gender differences in the way people communicated with those who had offended them. When men try to forgive, they do so by having face-to-face conversations. By contrast, women are more likely to initiate the process of forgiveness in multiple ways, using letters, phone calls, and third-party involvement, in addition to face-to-face interactions.

Gender differences also depended on the relationship the victim had with the violator. In our study, when we grouped the categories of spouse/partner, children, and extended family together, women reported that 60 percent of harms that are difficult or impossible to forgive occur within the family. By contrast, men reported a 45 percent occurrence in the family and 31 percent within a work context. For women, events related to work relationships were cited only 20 percent of the time. This raises some interesting questions. Are violations that happen to women most likely to occur within family relationships? Or do women simply find violations within family more painful and therefore more difficult to forgive? Perhaps the traditional breadwinner role for men makes workplace violations more important for them. Both of these findings suggest that gender differences in regard to forgiveness are subtle.

# Forgiveness Is Learned and Practiced in Loving Relationships

Because parents are crucial models for behavior, our early family experiences affect our ability to forgive. Since even the healthiest family life is marked by a series of hurts and repairs, our first lessons about forgiveness occur at home. As children, we observed adults both forgiving others and being forgiven. In our sample, approximately half the subjects came from families where people practiced forgiveness. Adults not only modeled it for their children, but they also required it of them. As Linda reported,

> I had three sisters; one was always annoying another, from borrowing a favorite hairbrush to insulting a boyfriend. My mother didn't let us go to bed until we had settled our issues. Eventually, that practice became a lifelong habit.

Linda recognized that her own ease with forgiveness grew out of the requirements her mother had imposed on her in childhood.

Beyond our relationships with parents and other caregivers, the possibility of forgiveness is enhanced by positive communication with other people who are important to us. In relationships where communication is respectful and empathic, neural pathways develop in response to daily habits of communication. Subconscious habits of reflection and dialogue build relationships where forgiveness is more likely to occur.

Forgiveness may be practiced in rituals, rather than words. Florists would have less business if sending flowers were not a well-understood method of asking for forgiveness. Preprinted cards requesting forgiveness suggest that even in the age of cell phones and the Internet, mailing an "I'm sorry" message is believed by many to be effective. Whether the apology prompts forgiveness then becomes the decision of the one who receives it.

Our willingness to commit to the future of a relationship and our level of closeness with a person who has harmed us are key aspects of whether we choose to forgive. Typically, people are more likely to apologize and forgive another if they have sufficient investment in the relationship. Most married people who discover their partner's infidelity are initially devastated. Some will opt to divorce their spouse because of that significant breach of trust. Others will decide that there are more compelling reasons to remain married and will forgive the offense.

## The Influence of Relative Power in the Workplace

In the workplace, our decisions about forgiveness are influenced by relative power. Researchers Karl Acquino, Thomas M. Tripp, and Robert J. Bies describe how these decisions are made.[7] First, we estimate who has relatively more power in a situation. If the person who harms us is higher in the organizational hierarchy than we are, chances are that we will consider our options carefully and probably choose to ignore or downplay the offense in order to maintain a relationship with our supervisor or manager. On the other hand, those same managers and executives make decisions that tilt in the other direction. That is, higher-status people feel pressure to assert their authority when harmed by a person of lower status. In terms of how we think about relative power in the workplace, the employee asks, "What can I do?" while the higher-status boss wonders, "What should I do?"

In the first instance of relative power, typically the lower-power person does not take revenge himself but looks to organizational avenues, such as the Equal Employment Opportunity Commission, to address a wrong committed by a higher-status person. However, the higher-status person generally seeks retaliation, rather than forgiveness, on the grounds that an aggressive response is necessary to reinforce the status quo. Thus, the lower-status person has greater motivation to forgive offenses than do those of higher status in the organization.

> The time is always right to do what is right.
>
> —MARTIN LUTHER KING JR.

## Reciprocity, Fairness, and Justice Spur Forgiveness

In our experience as mediators, we find it is helpful to remind offended clients of the times when they themselves have erred and been forgiven. We ask questions like these: "What do you think the other person could be feeling about this transgression?" or "How do you feel when you've made a mistake and must apologize?" These remind the offending party that we are all subject to error and that apologizing usually involves some embarrassment and loss of face.

The offender may also embrace the concept of reciprocity. As mediators, we know that inviting one party to consider the perspective of the other is critical to working toward a mutually satisfying resolution. Mediators may guide the person crafting an apology by asking, "How would a person in such a circumstance feel?" or "How would you feel if it happened to you?"

Acknowledging our own failure can promote a deeper understanding of another's failure. Reciprocity can be a good first step in repairing a relationship. Hundreds of years ago, Lord George Herbert made the point that forgiveness is a bridge to repairing relationships.

> He that cannot forgive others breaks the bridge over which he must pass himself if he would ever reach heaven; for every man has a need to be forgiven.[8]

In addition to reciprocity, a sense of fairness is important in forgiveness. Many cultures embrace the notion that a serious offense may be repaired by requiring restitution of some kind from the offender. Depending on the culture, the law, or the relationship, restitution might be material, psychological, or some combination of the two. Sometimes the offended people demand restitution; sometimes they are satisfied with an apology. Occasionally, a change of behavior will restore the relationship. Underlying all these choices is the understanding that an offender making restitution restores peace to both individuals and community.

Medical errors provide interesting examples of the importance of justice. Patients who have suffered as a result of physician or hospital malpractice often demand justice. In the past, lawyers representing doctors and medical systems have advised their clients against offering apologies to patients for fear that words of regret might suggest legal liability. On the contrary, studies find that when medical practitioners acknowledge mistakes, it reduces resentment and the likelihood of legal action by patients and their families. This reduction in malpractice claims against doctors who are willing to apologize has led some states to pass legislation that makes those apologies inadmissible in malpractice suits. In these states, cases involving medical errors are generally settled in less costly and more timely ways than through the courts.[9]

While the drive for fairness encourages forgiveness among individuals, within organizational settings people often seek procedural justice.

Employees who feel wronged may not seek to exact revenge if they believe the organization will resolve the problem fairly. Procedural justice involves the mechanisms through which organizations address offenses committed in the workplace. Of course, simply having procedures in place, such as a dispute resolution system, is not sufficient. They also must be fairly applied.

A large university spent a year designing a conflict resolution system that would give students, faculty, and staff a systematic way to address grievances. But when a faculty member who was denied tenure chose to seek redress through the grievance system, her contract was terminated. The university reports that no one has used the system since. When managers implement a fair process of conflict resolution, employees feel fairness is ensured and they are less likely to engage in revenge or avoidance.

While general norms, such as equity, reciprocity, and justice, are found in many cultures, there are also core values specific to particular cultures. People may even reject material compensation when asked to drop their commitment to their deepest values and will defend them, regardless of the costs. For instance, Israelis and Palestinians were asked about trading land for peace, a concept that most Westerners find perfectly acceptable. Across the political spectrum, however, almost all Israelis and Palestinians surveyed rejected this trade-off, citing sacred values such as "full sovereignty over Jerusalem," or "recognition of nation" and "right of return." Even more interesting, the greater the monetary incentive, the greater the disgust from respondents, who said, "No, we do not sell ourselves for any amount!"[10] The business model of negotiation is clearly not appropriate in this conflict.

> It's a strange truth, but forgiveness is a painful and difficult process. It's not something that happens overnight. It's an evolution of the heart.
>
> —SUE MONK KIDD

However, in the same situation, other norms facilitate forgiveness and promote peace. For instance, Hamas absolutists who rejected financial offers for sacred land were later inclined to accept deals that involved their enemies making symbolic gestures. An official apology for Palestinian suffering in the 1967 war is one example suggested by Hamas members as a path to forgiveness. Similarly, Israeli respondents were willing to make concessions based on explicit recognition of Israel's right to exist by

Hamas. Progress on culturally specific sacred values might open the way for negotiations that have failed on the basis of material trade-offs.[11]

## Healing National Violence

Nations may choose to practice forgiveness when revenge would be a more traditional approach. For instance, South Africa chose to use a Truth and Reconciliation Commission to investigate human rights abuses at the end of the apartheid era in the 1990s and El Salvador did the same at the end of its civil war in 1992. Nelson Mandela argued that South African citizens would benefit more from the telling of atrocity stories and eliciting forgiveness than they would from judicial action against individuals found to be guilty of those atrocities. Since then, the United States Institute of Peace has documented more than twenty other nations that have used Truth and Reconciliation Commissions following civil war. These commissions exemplify how nations have invented and employed social tools to promote forgiveness and civil peace in the future.

Scholar Rajeev Bhargava notes that a post-traumatic society choosing collective healing over revenge or punishment must remember the past in two ways. First, there must be assurances that crimes associated with the past may not recur without liability for future perpetrators. Secondly, memorials such as the Atomic Dome in Hiroshima and the Holocaust museum in Washington, D.C., must educate present and future citizens about the evils of the past. It is difficult to persuade a national government to memorialize its errors but those that do promote healing and facilitate forgiveness.[12]

Strangely, forgiveness may be more readily achieved in authoritarian cultures than in democratic societies. Writing about the 1994 genocide of Tutsis by Hutus, a local political scientist notes that Rwandans share a culture of unquestioning deference. He believes the slaughter only became widespread when officials organized meetings and radio broadcasts that directed Hutu citizens to kill fellow citizens who were Tutsi. In this culture of obedience, neighbors, as well as husbands and wives, began killing each other in the most heinous ways.

The year 2014 marked remembrance of the *gutsembatsemba*, or "radical extermination," Rwanda's genocide. Writing in the *New York Times*, Jean-Marie Kamatali reports that the killing of Tutsis by Hutus was one of the worst episodes of human depravity since the Holocaust:

At no other time in the history of our species were so many of us killed so fast or so intimately. Roughly a million people in a hundred days, most of them butchered by hand, by neighbors, with household tools and homemade weapons—machetes and hoes and hammers and clubs.[13]

Twenty years later, some Rwandans are pursuing ongoing efforts to achieve reconciliation, working closely with the Association Modeste et Innocent, the Rwandan branch of Pax Christi, the international Catholic peace movement. Small groups of Hutus and Tutsis are counseled over many months, until a perpetrator of violence makes a formal request for forgiveness to the victim. If the survivor grants forgiveness, the perpetrator and his family typically bring the survivor's family a basket of offerings, generally food and beer. The accord is sealed with song and dance.

After this process, a variety of interactions between victims and perpetrators may be observed. Some pairs sit together speaking easily. Others have no interest in further communication. Varying degrees of forgiveness and willingness to reconcile are quite evident and understandable.

Rwanda also arrested many perpetrators; at least 14,000 Hutus have been imprisoned and tried. Defendants explained to their attorneys that, regardless of their guilt, they should not have to suffer severe sentences because they were only following orders. This did not reflect the sentences later handed down, but it does represent the thinking of obedience cultures. Strange but logical, the culture of obedience promotes forgiveness as well as injustice. For example, when a judge asked one Tutsi survivor whether she could truly forgive the murderer of her children, she replied, "The government forgave them. What can I do? I also forgave him." Unquestioning deference underlay both the slaughter and the forgiveness that followed.

## There Is No Simple, Singular Answer

The question of who will be forgiving has multiple answers. For individuals, measures of both physical and psychological health are correlated with the tendency to forgive. Even though we lack convincing evidence that education, age, or gender alone predict who will or won't forgive others, gender studies do indicate that men and women go about pursuing forgiveness in different ways. Evidence suggests that a religious or spiritual inclination predisposes people toward forgiveness. Children who observe forgiveness practiced in their families of origin and who are consistently reinforced in the practice are more likely to grow up to be forgiving adults.

Finally, justice, reciprocity, and fairness are widely occurring social norms that encourage forgiveness. Other norms may be culturally specific. Rituals reinforce community norms and provide socially acceptable paths of forgiveness. Consistent social messages promote the value of forgiveness and its practice.

## Questions

1. Is there any offense that is unforgivable? If so, what is it?

2. How did those in your family of origin practice forgiveness? Or did they just ignore issues requiring forgiveness?

3. How do your religious beliefs align with your practice of forgiveness?

4. What do you consider the most important aspect of a situation in deciding whether or not to forgive someone for a serious offense?

5. Describe typical practices of forgiveness that you see in your community.

CHAPTER 6

# THE PATH TO FORGIVENESS

## ACKNOWLEDGING OUR MISTAKES AND TAKING ACTION

> You may not cancel all the events that happen to you,
> but you can decide not to be reduced by them.
>
> —Maya Angelou

Even if we endorse forgiveness, we may not know how to achieve it. What is the right direction to take? What are the right words to say? Learning how to forgive is challenging. For example, Susan, one of our survey participants, described her struggle:

> I'm having a hard time forgiving my sister. We've been friends for life. However, our friendship changed recently. She quit responding to my letters and phone calls when she began spending time with our drug-dependent brother. I miss my sister, but I don't know if I can forgive her for letting me down to spend so much time with him.

On the surface, it seems as if Susan is developing bitterness and resentment toward her sister. But behind these negative feelings, Susan recently went through a difficult divorce and her business was having problems. She desperately needs the support and friendship of her sister, but now feels abandoned. Susan's inability to accept her own personal failures is interwoven with a growing resentment about the loss of her sister's friendship. Her ability to forgive her sister is linked to her ability to forgive herself for her own failures.

## Forgiveness Is a Journey

Some people make a conscious decision to forgive and simply do it. Then they go on with life and let go of the past. But most of us cannot do this. For many people, forgiveness comes slowly, like a journey measured in days, months, or years. Our relationship to the person who hurts us and the nature of the offense influence the length of this process.

For many people, the forgiveness journey is a series of peaks and valleys. At the peaks we experience moments of feeling better about things, but we descend into the valleys when something is said that triggers uncomfortable memories. Eventually, with practice and reflection, the peaks become less high and the valleys less deep. The forgiveness journey is much like healing from grief. At first, someone who experiences a loss will feel deep anger, abandonment, or disappointment, but over time the emotions diminish in intensity.

> To understand all is to forgive all.
> —BUDDHA

Jessica complained about her spouse's demeaning treatment of her over their many years of marriage and raising children. The emotional pain of living with her husband finally drove her to leave him. She said, "His treatment crushed my self-esteem." Jessica went through a divorce, then spent some time at a retreat center, and eventually built a new, healthy relationship with another man. She slowly forgave her first husband for the way he'd treated her. As she explains, "Forgiveness was gradual, almost as subtle as the process of trees changing from winter barrenness to leafing out in the spring. I couldn't define a moment when it occurred, but over time I could see it had happened." She describes how both she and her new husband were even able to establish a friendship with this first husband. On her journey, Jessica traveled through separation, reflection, growth, prayer, and healing.

## The Philosophy behind Forgiveness

Martin Luther King Jr., pastor and civil rights activist, preached, "We must develop and maintain the capacity to forgive. He who is devoid of the power to forgive is devoid of the power of love."[1] Ideally, we know we are imperfect beings and attempt to rise above the desire for revenge after we've been harmed. We seek to be strong enough to acknowledge and express our anger toward the person who has harmed us, but also strong enough to put that anger behind us. King called this "preemptive mercy." This attitude of understanding encourages the offender to seek forgiveness.

Next let's take a hard look at the circumstances that gave rise to various offenses and consider how someone who offends can remediate them. Journalist David Brooks offers examples of the way harms may be categorized and responded to:

> Some sins, like anger and lust, are like wild beasts. They have to be fought through habits of restraint. Some sins like bigotry are like stains. They can only be expunged by apology and cleansing. Some like stealing are like a debt. They can only be rectified by repaying. Some, like adultery, are more like treason than like crime; they can only be rectified by slowly reweaving relationships.[2]

After the offender has decided on a course of action like the ones listed above, she must engage in self-criticism and confession. As offenders, we must be willing to endure a period of inward shame and outward disgrace. Finally, there is the possibility of reconciliation and renewed trust. King argued that both sinner and sinned against are stronger for initiating and sustaining the search for forgiveness. He also believed that the process strengthened the social fabric, thereby building a healthier community.

Jesuit writers Dennis, Sheila, and Matthew Linn agree that while there may be the occasional miracle, normally we arrive at forgiveness through predictable phases. The authors argue that the stages of forgiveness parallel the five stages of grief posited by Elizabeth Kübler-Ross.[3]

| Five Stages | | |
|---|---|---|
| STAGE | DYING | FORGIVENESS |
| Denial | There's still a chance | I wasn't really hurt that badly. |
| Anger | It's the doctor's fault | Look at the agony she's caused! |
| Bargaining | Set up conditions | I can't forgive unless he apologizes. |
| Depression | I neglected my health | I should have known not to trust her. |
| Acceptance | Death brings a release | I will become a stronger person and experience personal growth as a result of this challenge. |

The Linns write that each of the forgiveness stages is "... like a chapter in a story, revealing part of ourselves that we are tempted to push away. When we listen respectfully to all five chapters in the story of a hurt, we regain our center and a creative solution can emerge naturally."[4] This overview of the phases of forgiveness prepares us to pursue the communication tools associated with successful forgiveness.

## Communicating the Desire for Forgiveness

Most of us seek forgiveness when we acknowledge mistakes we've made that have harmed others. In our survey we asked people if they had sought the forgiveness of others when they committed a wrong. Amazingly, 80 percent of those surveyed believed that they had tried to make amends. Of those who did seek forgiveness, 39 percent chose face-to-face meetings, 7 percent wrote letters or sent a card, and 7 percent sent emails or used social media to request forgiveness. The rest of those 80 percent did not specify how they attempted to communicate how sorry they felt.

> Always forgive your enemies—nothing annoys them so much.
>
> —OSCAR WILDE

Relationships have a great deal to do with what strategy we choose to repair the harm done. For example, in a work setting, an explanation or acknowledgment of the mistake may be sufficient to repair the relationship. But with a family member or in another close personal relationship, an apology, recommitment to the relationship, and personal assurance that no harm was intended may be necessary to restore trust and safety in the relationship.

The choice of strategy tends to fall into two categories, either direct or indirect.

| DIRECT | DESCRIPTION |
|---|---|
| Apology | Express contrition and a commitment to repair damage. |
| Explanation | Specify why the harm was committed. |
| Expression of regret | Voice remorse about the harm committed. |
| Dialogue | Discuss factors that led up to or contributed to the harm done. |
| Acknowledgement | Acknowledge the harm and accept responsibility for it. |

| INDIRECT | DESCRIPTION |
|---|---|
| Humor | Lower tensions or minimize the significance of the harm through humor. |
| Restitution | Do something for the offended person or give a gift as an act of contrition. |
| Change behavior | Practice good behavior designed to communicate your willingness to change. |
| Hugs/touch | Offer nonverbal expressions of appreciation to restore trust. |
| Emotion | Demonstrate contrition by tears or sadness. |

Communication scholars Douglas Kelley and Vincent Waldron conducted a study that examined the effectiveness of forgiveness-seeking strategies.[5] The researchers contend that discussions that seek forgiveness are most effective when the communication displays the following:

- Unfolds in a way that reduces uncertainty
- Allows partners to save face
- Builds confidence that the offensive behavior will not recur

## Acknowledge the Harm

Admission of harm is a good first step in seeking forgiveness. Acknowledgment demonstrates that the offender is committed to the relationship and invites the offended person to believe that the offender deserves another chance. Acknowledging wrongdoing also brings to the surface how much the offended person currently values the relationship. An unwillingness to forgive may signal deeper issues in the relationship that require more than seeking forgiveness for a single offense.

## Make Your Intentions Clear

An important second step is to clarify your intention. When someone believes that another was intentionally trying to do him harm, forgiveness can be nearly impossible to achieve. A person seeking forgiveness needs to reduce the perception that she had any intention to do harm, if that was the case. Clarifying intentions may involve statements like these:

- I was not aware that what I said would do you harm.
- I didn't mean to do you harm. That was not my intention.

- I was trying to be funny. I had no idea that you might take offense at my attempt at humor.
- I did that without thinking. I'm so sorry that it upset you.

Clarifying your intention may be as an important as making an apology and in some cases may replace an apology. Chronic distrust in relationships is often fueled by a belief that one of the partners intends to cause the other emotional harm. In this case, we might hear statements such as, "That's why he says those things" or "That's why she behaves the way she does." The person seeking forgiveness needs to clarify his intentions and remove any doubt as to his motives.

# Granting Forgiveness

We get a much different picture when we consider how often others have asked us for our forgiveness. Of those we surveyed, less than half the respondents said that offenders asked for forgiveness. Of the offenders who did make attempts, 24 percent chose face-to-face approaches, 5 percent chose email, and only 8 percent placed phone calls. Our participants did not tell us any other methods that were used. Comparing these results to self-reported forgiveness seeking (80 percent), we are reminded that we tend to recall our own behavior more positively than that of others.

The reasons someone might not want to grant forgiveness when the offender has reached out to repair harm done include the offender's:

- Unwillingness to admit fault
- Fear of punishment
- Lack of commitment to the relationship
- Denial that any harm was done
- Guilt or shame that the offender does not want to deal with

## The Readiness Factor

Oftentimes, we are not able to forgive another until we are ready. Being ready involves one or more of the following preconditions.

1. Being calm enough to think about the harm rationally. If our emotions are on high alert, it's difficult to devote our full attention to understanding the dynamics of what has occurred.

2. Developing a clear understanding of what our emotions are linked to. Lack of clarity about feelings can make enduring emotions difficult to resolve. What do I need? What am I missing?

3. Gaining a clear understanding about the action that triggered the emotional reaction. Ask, "Why does this bother me?"

4. Separating the current harm from memories of past harms. A reaction to an event that occurs today may actually be a reaction to events from months or even years ago. Ask yourself, "What is the real issue here?"

5. Deciding how important the harm is. Does the harm require further conversation or is it insignificant enough to let it go? Sometimes the tension triggered by others is related more to us than it is to them. We may be tired, stressed by work, or overwhelmed by all that we have to do. The offender just happens to be at the wrong place at the wrong time and becomes the target of our frustration.

For example, Bob borrowed a lawnmower from his neighbor Adam. Several weeks later Bob gave the lawnmower back with a broken blade. Irritated, Adam asked Bob about the blade. Bob responded, "The blade had a crack in it when I got it. I'm not responsible for it breaking." Adam became angry and accused Bob of being irresponsible. Their angry exchange became the source of a grudge that lasted for years. If we apply the principles specified above, we might ask Adam to delay his conversation with Bob until he calmed down,

> You make yourself and others suffer just as much when you take offense as when you give offense.
>
> —KEN KEYES JR.

identified what he felt, and figured out what bothered him. He needed to consider whether this was a pattern of behavior that Bob displayed or an isolated incident. It might have been helpful for Adam to consider whether the cost of this blade was worth the loss of a relationship.

Another aspect of readiness is the time needed to recover from serious harm, the term physicians use to describe a natural return to health: *tincture of time*. Several years ago in central Colorado, David, a college sophomore, was killed when a vehicle driven by his roommate Dylan ran off the road and crashed. Neither the driver nor the other teens in the back seat were seriously injured. All had been drinking, but the driver was convicted and sentenced to prison, having just passed his eighteenth birthday.

Sandy, David's mother, was shocked, sorrowful, and angry at the tragedy that took her son's life. For many months she and David's siblings directed their anger at Dylan, the driver. They were so miserable they eventually turned to a grief counselor to help them resolve their anguish at the loss of their son and brother. In the counseling process, they realized that Dylan had also been harmed. Earlier he had reached out to them, but phone messages from him and his parents were not returned; Sandy was just not ready to hear from him, much less extend forgiveness.

With the aid of a mediator, Dylan met with his deceased friend's family and was finally able to express his own sorrow and repentance in person. Sandy and the surviving children were able to honor and accept Dylan's appeal for forgiveness. They attempted to continue the contact while he was in prison and, following his release several years later, they have spoken together publicly about the power of dialogue in achieving forgiveness.[6]

## Discussing the Harm

In granting forgiveness, most people choose a direct strategy of saying, "I forgive you." However, just saying the words *I forgive you* may not give either party sufficient closure to get over the harm done. Indirect strategies of humor, leaving it alone and hoping it will go away, or downplaying the problem also may not be sufficient. Oftentimes, some conversation needs to occur about the event that caused the harm and the effect the action had on the one who was harmed. Otherwise, the one harmed may store up the memory of the harm to be used in a later discussion. At one time or another, most of us have been involved in discussions where we've heard about things we've done months or years ago. Memory of the past harm could be used to justify an act of revenge by the one who was harmed. "He cheated on me and this is my way of getting even." A forgiveness discussion allows resentment to surface and reassures both parties that the event is past history with no chance of it occurring again.

## Acknowledging the Role of Grace

In a discussion about granting forgiveness, it is important to incorporate the spiritual concept of grace. Grace is unconditional and unmerited acceptance. We care about others not because they deserve it but because we choose to extend benevolence or compassion to them. We each possess a circle of grace that surrounds us. For some, that circle might be small—only a few friends or family members. We readily choose to forgive these people because they are closest to us and we tend to understand them best. But we each possess the capacity to widen our circle of grace to influence the lives of others, such as when we extend forgiveness to the colleague whose delay caused us to miss a critical deadline. Widening our circle of grace enables us to make significant differences in the lives of those around us.

Some wrongdoing becomes difficult to forgive because the harm may trigger a complex swell of emotions. If disappointment were the only emotion we experienced, we might deal with the infraction swiftly through indirect forgiveness strategies. "Oh, it's okay, no big deal." However, forgiving a parent for abuse or abandonment might require the healing of feelings associated with diminished self-worth, lack of safety, anger, resentment, and bitterness. Personal repair may call for several linked healing journeys, not just one.

A deputy police chief tells a story of how grace and forgiveness transformed a potentially harmful situation. Several years ago, he pulled over a sixteen-year-old boy on a motorcycle. The boy was going fast enough that a ticket would have meant a large fine, probably paid for by his parents, and suspension of his license because of his age. The boy was scared to death as the deputy chief initiated a conversation with him. He offered the boy a choice: he could take the ticket and go home, understanding the consequences, or he could call his parents on his cell phone and let the police officer talk to them. The boy chose to call his parents. The deputy chief said to the mother, "I can give your boy a ticket and he will lose his license or you can work with him to drive within the speed limit." She replied, "I'll work with him and you won't see him speeding again." The police officer recognized that suspending the boy's license would make him resentful toward police for the rest of his life. Granting him grace, with the help of the boy's mother, stood

> Parts of us cry out for settlement, not with anyone else, but within ourselves. Is the old anger worth it? In solitude we come to peace with the life behind us.
>
> —JOAN CHITTISTER

the best chance of changing the boy's behavior. The deputy chief made a choice between forgiving the offense and strictly enforcing the law.

### Understanding the Actions of the Offender

Stanford psychologist Fred Luskin contends that in some cases granting forgiveness can heal us, if we depersonalize the harm committed and try to understand what lay behind the actions of the offender.[7] This is not to trivialize our hurt or discount the significance of harmful behavior. Rather, it is to point out that certain people may not be aware of their actions. Some people may act without thinking or without the intention of doing harm. Others are so preoccupied with worry, tension, and doubts in their own lives that they are not aware that their actions are causing pain in the lives of others. In these cases, mercy, understanding, and compassion may go further than judgment. Forgiveness may be a gift that helps the perpetrator recover his better nature.

Asking for forgiveness isn't always easy. It begins with recognizing your own emotional issues and acknowledging that you said or did things that you did not intend. Using the words *I apologize* or *I'm sorry* is a crucial part of asking for forgiveness. Even though forgiveness occurs, you may not hear the phrase *You are forgiven*. What matters is that you've faced and dealt with a problem you created. Asking for forgiveness involves several steps:

> Step 1: Recognize your harmful behavior. You did or said something that harmed another.
>
> Step 2: Identify what might have contributed to your behavior, such as being stressed.
>
> Step 3: Build up your courage and offer an apology. Say the words *I'm sorry*.
>
> Step 4: Pause, stop talking, and allow the other person to respond.
>
> Step 5: If it's important for you to hear forgiveness verbally expressed, ask, "Will you forgive me?"

# Forgetting Begins with Forgiving

Humans are hardwired to remember their past. Oftentimes, the memories that cause us distress are those when we were harmed. Those memories can protect us from similar harm. However, memories of harm we've sustained can also trap us in emotional cycles of sadness and disappointment. Our thoughts become enmeshed in our brain's circuitry, which loops around and around and back to the same place.

Research suggests that if we move down the path of forgiveness, we are better able to forget—not forget entirely, but enough to diminish the negative emotions associated with a past event. If we are going to forget, however, we must begin with forgiveness. Forgiveness takes the sting out of negative emotions so that they can heal.

Based on the work of psychologist Everett Worthington, there are several ways to help manage the process of forgetting while forgiving.[8]

1. **Decondition yourself.** When you begin to think of an uncomfortable event from your past, tell yourself, "I'm not going there. That was then and this is now. I've learned a great deal about myself since then and I'm not going to let those memories have any effect on me now." Some people choose to wear a rubber band on their wrists. When a painful memory surfaces, they snap the rubber band. This interrupts the thinking they want to change. As you adjust your thinking, your mind creates new memory circuits, which replace the old patterns.

2. **Stop the self-criticism.** We accomplish little by allowing old memories to blame us for not being perfect or for expecting us to please everyone around us. That's not healthy or appropriate. We can't be everything to everyone. We don't have the power to manage our impulses throughout life. We will make mistakes and we will let people down. You're not expected to do it all. Tell yourself, "I will accept myself with flaws. I don't have to be perfect to be okay. I will be kind and gracious toward myself. If I can't take care of myself, how can I be expected to take care of others? I will speak to myself as a good friend."

3. **Focus on the positive.** Our mind is predisposed to remember failure and negative experiences in life. We can counter that predisposition by focusing on positive experiences. If you feel guilt about letting someone down, replace that memory with one of when that person smiled or enjoyed your presence. Put memories of the good times in place of the ones that pull you down.

4. **Give it to God or the Sacred.** For those with a spiritual orientation, one of the actions that can provide the greatest freedom is to give the bad memories and life failures to God. By surrendering to divine compassion, we grant ourselves the gifts of grace and peace.

Seeking forgiveness and granting forgiveness are intimately connected. Our lack of acceptance of others may be connected to our lack of acceptance of ourselves. To strengthen both, we need to widen our circle of grace. We can monitor our expectations and ask ourselves, "Can this be less than perfect and still be okay?" We can choose to be more accepting of mistakes that others make as well as our own. We can ask ourselves, "What will it take to make this right?" Grace is extended both outward to others and inward to ourselves.

> Know all and you will pardon all.
>
> —Thomas à Kempis

## Questions

1. Where are you on the forgiveness journey with respect to some hurts in your life? Just beginning, down the road a bit, or at the end and seeking closure?

2. What is it within you that makes you want to hold on to unpleasant memories?

3. What would it take for you to forgive and let go, understanding that this doesn't mean you have to reconcile with the person who harmed you?

4. What would it take for you to extend mercy and benevolence to someone who harmed you in the past?

5. What is the connection between asking for forgiveness and forgiving others in your life?

# CHAPTER 7

# SELF-FORGIVENESS

## CONFRONTING OUR HARSHEST CRITIC

> Holding on to anger is like grasping a hot
> coal with the intent of throwing it at someone
> else; you are the one who gets burned.
>
> —Buddha

F orgiveness involves three dimensions: forgiving others, being forgiven by others, and forgiving yourself. This third dimension may be the most difficult one. You live with memories of words or actions that date back decades. Many of the people you've harmed may no longer be part of your life; some of them may have passed away. Self-forgiveness involves letting go of these old disappointments and failures. This chapter covers the sources of those difficulties and uncovers ways you can open yourself to the acceptance of forgiveness. We are not advising you to ignore the voice of conscience: this chapter simply addresses the lingering discomfort that persists even though you have taken the appropriate steps toward seeking forgiveness.

## Distinguishing Guilt, Shame, Disappointment, and Regrets

A complex web of emotions plagues us when we are struggling with self-forgiveness. Identifying these emotions may help us move forward toward healing.

## Guilt

Guilt is the feeling you have when you disappoint yourself and/or others. As humans, we do not always act in ways that reflect our best nature; our natural flaws ensure that we will need to self-assess and self-correct our behavior from time to time. For instance, you would feel guilty if you posted an embarrassing picture of your former partner on Facebook. Then there was the tempting moment when your computer-savvy roommate found the history test answers online and both of you used them to advantage. Conscience responds to such mistakes by inducing guilt feelings. If guilt is not addressed, you will continue to experience difficulty with self-forgiveness.

## Shame

Shame is a negative feeling that you internalize, based on past events or treatment by others. Shame arises not from specific events but from a sense of self that is unworthy. Sometimes shame arises from your own behavior; for example, you take an action for which you feel guilty, such as "I cheated on a test," and generalize it to "I'm a cheater." At other times, the shame may be rooted in how you were treated by important others, such as parents or caregivers, who criticized you so regularly that your self-image reflects their negative views. Community experiences may also be a source of shame. For instance, someone who is obese may incorporate a sense of low self-worth and shame from negative reactions he gets in public life. Shame may be so deeply ingrained that you need help from a pastor or counselor as you work through it toward self-forgiveness.

## Disappointment

Disappointment related to self is the emotion you feel when you fall short of your own self-image. You disappoint yourself when you do not meet your own standards or those internalized from the expectations of significant others. You remember the gossip you passed on about a classmate who was thought to be "sleeping around," but being a gossip is not part of your self-image, so the memory disappoints and disturbs you. You didn't visit your aunt in the hospital before she passed away, even though you are usually quite responsive to family needs. When these memories recur often, they signal a continuing conflict between the self that disappointed you and the self that you wish to embrace. Such conflicts stand in the way of self-forgiveness.

## *Regrets*

Regrets are feelings you experience when you rethink decisions made in your past. Some regrets stem from your own action or lack of it. The older woman may think wistfully of the children she was not be able to have and regret her decision not to adopt. A middle-aged man may regret not changing careers when it became apparent that he was not going to be promoted to management. Regret about decisions you failed to make easily morphs into self-blame that interferes with self-forgiveness and creates difficulties in coming to terms with your past.

Other regrets relate to circumstances you could not control. Many of our survey participants felt the actions of their parents were the most difficult to forgive. Removed in time and place from their inadequate parents, they were still psychologically enmeshed in their childhood situation. Abuse or emotional neglect by one or more parents creates significant difficulties when it comes to forgiveness because, as children, we were powerless to change our circumstances. Adults who are still trying to please an impossible parent most likely will fail to meet that parent's expectations and then blame themselves as well as the parent. Regretting the childhood you didn't have gets in the way of self-forgiveness.

## Struggling with Shame

Sometimes high standards for performance rise to unreachable levels and become the practice of perfectionism. Eli, one of our survey participants, tells the story of his self-inflicted shame when he discovered that his son was gay. Active in his evangelical church, he "knew" that such behavior was sinful and that his son would no longer be welcome in the religious community that meant so much to Eli. What was seen by his church as deviant behavior did not accord with Eli's images of himself or his family members. Eli was ashamed to admit this, but also conflicted by the deep love he felt toward his son. The father's sense of morality did not reflect the reality of his son's life. At some point Eli will need to resolve this dilemma because he and his son want to resume a meaningful relationship.

Eli's example suggests another source of shame that prevents self-forgiveness. Community norms specify what is shameful and what is not. Some primitive tribes think nothing of women appearing partially naked, while in other cultures women must cover every body part. Agreement about what is shameful varies, but communities have strong feelings about what they hold to be shameful and strictly enforce these beliefs. Where community agreement is socially reinforced, guilt may easily morph into shame. Eli's sense of disgrace regarding his son's sexual orientation was more intense because of the strict norms of his religious community.

Shame related to community practices changes historically. Attitudes toward those who identify as lesbian, gay, bisexual, transgender, queer, or intersexed have evolved dramatically in the last decade in the United States. As community practices and legal strictures change, individuals have an opportunity to shift their own thinking and behavior as well. Perhaps this shift will result in a reassessment of past intolerance and a sense of guilt or regret for prejudice based on sexual preferences.

Another example of change in cultural practices concerns institutionalized racism, for which many of us feel shame. In the American South, during the nineteenth century and much of the twentieth century, African-Americans were segregated by law in every way imaginable: neighborhoods, schools, transportation, bathrooms, and water fountains, among others. These practices were outrageous and those who experienced white privilege during that time often feel guilty at their lack of sensitivity in retrospect.

Sometimes political leaders express guilt over racism both personally and publically. George Wallace was governor of Alabama in the 1960s; he is remembered as the villain of the civil rights era. At his first inauguration, he proclaimed "Segregation now, segregation tomorrow, segregation forever!"[1] While Alabama was not the only Southern state where violence erupted, the murder of the three Freedom Riders, Bloody Sunday (the first Selma march in 1965), and the church bombing where four little girls died all occurred in Alabama while Wallace was governor.

> Forgiveness of self is impossible until you stop longing for a better past.
>
> —ANONYMOUS

Later in life, George Wallace regretted the policies of bigotry that he had supported, and asked for forgiveness. Wallace repented and apologized to both political and religious leaders in the African-American community. Evidently his struggle for self-forgiveness was successful also. Those black leaders who became close to him afterward testify that his forgiveness of self and others was sincere. John Lewis, a black member of the U.S. Congress from

Georgia, who was born in Alabama, argues that Wallace's story reflects the inner transformation of a power-hungry politician into a child of God, looking to correct past wrongs. Not only did Wallace's words appear sincere but he also initiated programs to assist African-Americans in his last administration. Most convincing, he publically forgave Arthur Bremer, the man who attempted to assassinate him and left him crippled for life. Lewis comments on the intersection of the personal and the political:

> Our ability to forgive serves a higher moral purpose in our society. Through genuine repentance and forgiveness, the soul of our nation is redeemed.
>
> George Wallace deserves to be remembered for his effort to redeem his soul and in so doing mend the fabric of American society.[2]

Difficulty with self-forgiveness may also be linked to your distance from the person you have hurt. We hear repeatedly from people who feel blocked because they have lost touch with the injured party or, more difficult still, the harmed party has died. The inability to make a full apology to another often compounds the difficulty in forgiving ourself. In many of these cases, guilt is carried for years, sometimes even a lifetime.

The most painful instances of all seem to be those where the injuries to another result in suicide, especially of a young person. The following example came from LaToya, one of our graduate students who deeply regrets not standing up for a fellow student who was bullied:

> When I was in high school, there was a student who was constantly bullied for being different. For over a year, my fellow classmates made fun of Royce's clothes, mannerisms, and speech. His own so-called friends even made fun of him in social settings, which I am sure hurt more than the other students' bullying. The students had an agenda, which included bullying another student to make themselves feel bigger and better than someone else. Royce perceived their actions as a threat and became anxious. That anxiety, I'm sure, led him to be nervous constantly and feel unsafe in their environment. Royce was hurt by others' words and actions and felt alone in the situation.

Royce tried to speak out against the bullying and even went to the school's disciplinary board regarding the treatment he was receiving in the classroom. The disciplinary board did not recognize his classmates' behavior as bullying and did not take any action against the students involved. They stated that these actions were typical teenage behavior and they had not done anything that required school action. This allowed the students to continue their bullying because it was working and there were no perceived consequences. I feel that this was a critical part of this conflict and had the school board taken action, the dynamics in the situation could have changed drastically.

Shortly after the board's decision, Royce committed suicide. In his suicide note, he stated that he felt there was no way out and that not one single person cared what he was going through.

The actions of bullies are enabled by the passivity of bystanders. LaToya knows this and goes on to describe how her own failure to act in this instance has affected her long after high school. The guilt she felt at this young person's suicide preoccupies her mind, but his death seemingly leaves her no options for redress. Her sense of guilt appears to be blocked from the usual steps of making amends and seeking absolution.

Guilt, shame, disappointment, and regret are all obstacles to self-forgiveness. These feelings may arise from painful personal experiences in our family of origin, condemnation for what our society finds shameful, or the difficulty of apologizing to a victim. However, you can and should surmount those obstacles. As theologian Lewis Smedes explains, "We need to forgive ourselves because the part of us that gets blamed feels split off from the part that does the blaming."[3]

# The Search for Self-Forgiveness Begins with Sorting

Achieving self-forgiveness requires us to explore ways to manage impediments to self-forgiveness. The path to self-forgiveness begins by making three lists:

## List #1: Actions for Which You Are Guilty

Compose a list of actions and attitudes for which you are guilty. These are actions you took knowingly and for which you feel adult responsibility. If you find objective judgment difficult to reach, a counselor or some other trusted person may be consulted. In the previous chapter we focused on how to communicate with others so as to convey sorrow, recognition of the damage you have caused, and your intent to correct your behavior in the future. When these steps have been completed, you are ready to proceed with self-forgiveness.

## List #2: Specifying the Distortions

Account for incidents where you assumed more than your share of responsibility or distorted your role. For instance, in the example above, LaToya might reason that the teen's suicide was primarily the responsibility of adults on the school disciplinary board who ignored the gravity of Royce's complaints. Some call this "proportionate guilt." LaToya can use the incident as a prompt to take action the next time she encounters bullying, but she can also give herself a break in terms of the degree of personal responsibility she bears for Royce's suicide.

## List #3: What's Beyond Your Control

Document actions that were truly beyond your control and for which you wrongly charged yourself. The child who was molested is not responsible, no matter what she said or did to adults before that happened. Ray Rice's fiancée did not deserve to be beaten senseless in an elevator by the former Ravens football star.

Psychologist and *New York Times* best-selling author Richard Hanson offers insight into a Buddhist approach to the sorting process.[4] He recommends making three piles of behavior or events that seem to require self-forgiveness, but one of his piles is different than those in the lists described above. Hanson's first pile comprises moral faults. We must learn from these, take moral responsibility for them, and make amends for having caused harm. That appears to be similar to our first list. He calls the second list "unskillfulness" and emphasizes that this requires correction only. Hanson uses the example of gossip as an unskillful behavior. You take note of it, resolve to do better in the future, but make no more of it than that. Hanson's third list resembles ours, in that it segregates those acts for which, perfectionism notwithstanding, you are not responsible. Hanson also suggests making a written account, not only of the three piles but also acknowledging to yourself when you have taken responsibility and made amends. You need to look carefully at this account and appreciate those actions that allow you to release responsibility.

## Working through the Three Lists

Once the sorting is completed and you are satisfied that you have truly accounted for your actions in the first list, you can begin the process of discharging unwanted preoccupations in lists two and three. This basically happens through self-understanding and giving yourself the kind of compassion shown to you by loving others. Self-understanding starts with what Sidney Simon and Suzanne Simon call affirmations, such as, "I used to believe that I had to carry this load of guilt and shame for the rest of my life, but now I know that I have punished myself long enough, and can leave the self-blame stage."[5] Others use the term "inner critic" to describe that voice in your head that frequently finds you lacking and that focuses on occasional mistakes without taking into account consistent better behavior.

When you determine that the negative voice is not that of conscience, but that of your nagging inner critic, address your fears and vulnerabilities. Pay attention to signals that you need to take care of yourself, be comforted by trusted others, or just simply come up for air and look at your life in a less serious manner. If you seek reassurance from yourself, you can offer yourself the same comfort and forgiveness that a loving partner or parent has offered you in the past. You can regard yourself as more than just the harmful act that is troubling you. Remind yourself of positive qualities and actions for which you are known. Again, these suggestions will work best when you put them in writing; writing promotes the more objective stance that you need to take to quiet the inner critic.

> People have to learn to heal themselves, to take that damaged little child inside of them and make it better.
>
> —Marlo Thomas

If you are seeking forgiveness from someone who is inaccessible or has died, you can still write a letter expressing your sorrow and willingness to do better next time. LaToya can write to Royce, unload her guilt at her passivity, and express her regret over the tragic outcome. Even though the person you have harmed may be removed by distance or death and cannot read your words, expressing your distress and repentance in writing helps many to release regrets.

## Self-Awareness, Trusted Others, and Grace

Self-awareness plays a critical role in self-forgiveness. One of our clients offered an example of attaining self-forgiveness through close observation and deliberate choice. Deandra worked as a visiting nurse; corporate head-quarters dictated a tight schedule, requiring her to drive long distances to see patients. The work was highly stressful, and, compounding that, she found herself continually irritated by thoughtless drivers. She had no compunction about releasing her irritation by honking her horn. Occasionally, a particularly slow-moving motorist would receive an angry yell or a finger signal. At the end of the day, Deandra was not proud of herself or the aggression she had directed toward others on the road; she made many an unsuccessful resolution to reform.

Despite regrets and self-blame, Deandra's bad driving habits persisted.

As it happened, Deandra's sister developed ALS, a miserable illness that took her life in less than nine months. The deterioration and death of her only sibling was devastating. Deandra

> I think that if God forgives us, we must forgive ourselves. Otherwise, it's almost like setting ourselves up as a higher tribunal than Him.
>
> —C. S. Lewis

grieved deeply and possessed little energy for a lengthy period. As she began to emerge from her sad state, she noticed that she had been driving very differently; she simply didn't have the verve to honk and yell at other motorists when they annoyed her. Trained to observe the behavior of her patients, Deandra made an observation about herself. She had just spent a long time as a considerate driver; she reasoned that since she was capable of this unintentional behavioral change, she could also choose to behave this way. She did so and forgave herself for past offenses against fellow drivers.

If you are not successful at achieving self-forgiveness on your own, you can turn to others for help. Sometimes expressing your dissatisfaction with yourself to a partner or a trusted friend will break down barriers to self-forgiveness. Once a friend listened to us rant about our shortcomings and said, "Are you responsible for global warming, too?" That short, humorous sentence cut through months of regret and self-recrimination and we both laughed in relief.

Counselors and pastors are trained to help you work on self-forgiveness as well, as Charles experienced. Charles was a veteran of the wars in Iraq and Afghanistan. As a soldier on the front lines, he personally gunned down dozens of enemy soldiers and even some suspect civilians. In his efforts to deal with his intense guilt and remorse over his wartime actions, Charles tried everything, including counseling. But nothing helped, and he continued to live with a deep level of emotional pain.

Then one day he began attending a church, and after a year Charles decided to speak personally with the pastor. His tears flowed as he confessed his guilt and how he couldn't escape from it. At the end of the conversation, the pastor told him, "As far as the East is from the West, God removes this burden from you. God lets it all go. Now it's time for you to let it go."

As they prayed together, Charles realized that he was ready and he chose to let go of his anguish. At that moment he experienced a freedom he had not felt before. Although he knew he would never forget his actions during the war, now he could distance himself from those painful memories. For Charles, as for many others, self-forgiveness did not come easily, but was facilitated by pastoral understanding and response.

Your ability to forgive and be forgiven is closely linked to your ability to forgive yourself. Grace and patience with yourself tend to extend to other relationships. Forgiving yourself may involve various strategies, including:

- Granting yourself the same grace you are willing to grant others.
- Accepting that you are not perfect and that you make mistakes.
- Acknowledging that you've grown a great deal since you committed a particular offense and that you're not the same person now.
- Using self-talk to bolster your self-esteem, such as, "I am strong. I am better than I used to be. I know that I would behave differently now."
- Announcing to yourself that the debt for an offense has been paid through time served, contrition, or by a personal expression of grace.

Theologian Lewis Smedes adds that you can promote self-forgiveness through redemptive remembering.[6] Allow yourself to see a clearer picture of the past that includes the contributing actions of others or recognition of your lack of maturity or skills at the time you committed the offense. Let your current knowledge and experience provide a deeper understanding of past events. Who you are now is not who you were then. At a point like this, you begin to replace the negative emotions associated with the past—guilt, disappointment, anger, resentment, bitterness—with positive emotions, such as benevolence, compassion, grace. Say yes to a pardon granted to yourself for the past.

A colleague of ours offered a recent example of redemptive remembering that happened in her family of origin. A rift of three generations was repaired by the willingness of an uncle who decided to undo a lifetime of anger and self-blame. During the 1930s in Poland, Jacob saved considerable funds from his carpenter's work, hiding the money in his bedclothes. One day while he was at work, the money and his oldest son, Max, disappeared. It was later discovered that Max had immigrated to the United States, where he became a citizen and urged his whole family to join him. After the Nazis invaded Poland and began to place onerous restrictions on Jews, Jacob and his younger son Stephen joined Max in Chicago. Max sent them tickets and sponsored them for immigration to the United States; at that time, personal sponsorship was legally required before Jewish refugees could settle in the country. Max's mother and sister were reluctant to leave Poland and they were killed in Auschwitz.

> If you love God's gift of forgiveness more than you love your self-assessed righteousness, you know grace has visited you.
>
> —ANONYMOUS

Jacob was grateful for his son's generosity but Stephen never forgave his brother for stealing the money, even though it had been more than repaid by the cost of their tickets and resettlement. Max made abject apology for his theft, but Stephen's heart was hardened toward his brother. He moved away as soon as possible and never spoke to his brother again. His children were forbidden to make contact with their uncle and were told only about the theft of money, not the fact that Max had saved their father and grandfather's lives.

In his ninth decade, Stephen began to question the wisdom of his behavior toward his brother. Once he began this self-examination, it didn't take long for him to see Max's motivation for stealing the money and his foresight in leaving Poland while it was still possible. He could forgive his brother, but then blamed himself for fracturing their family all those years. His guilt over telling his children a partial version of the family history, his disappointment over his rigid thinking, and his regrets about the rift he'd caused in the family resulted in a heavy load of self-blame. So much time had passed that both Jacob and Max were long dead, and he did not know Max's surviving spouse or his children, whom he reasoned wouldn't want to hear from him anyway. Stephen felt stymied with self-blame at the end of his life and imagined no recourse.

> Remorse is the price we pay to forgive ourselves.
>
> —LEWIS SMEDES

Recently, a great niece conducting genealogy research for a college course discovered her uncle's contact information and contacted Stephen. Stephen saw the door to repairing family relationships suddenly open and he did not hesitate to walk through it. He immediately began to make amends for holding onto his resentment for so many years. He finally told his children the full story of Max's generosity in sponsoring their father's escape from Poland. He wrote to Max's surviving children, expressing his gratitude to his brother for saving his life. The niece's phone call was the trigger, but Stephen had prepared himself psychologically and was yearning for release. Self-forgiveness requires serious self-examination as well as the extension of compassion toward self and others, but in this case it finally happened.

There may not be a serendipitous phone call triggering self-forgiveness for you. However, you do not need to accept a lifetime practice of self-blame or the unrelenting recall of past mistakes. The suggestions above about how to forgive yourself and accept assistance from others have enabled many to break through resistance and offer themselves the same compassion they extend to others. Many of the practices described in chapter 6 and chapter 8 also apply to self-forgiveness and would prove useful to review. Self-forgiveness may be difficult, but with thought, time, and patience it is possible.

## ———————— Questions ————————

1. For which behaviors or attitudes do you find it most difficult to forgive yourself?

2. What past community practices seem shameful to you?

3. What does your inner critic say about your past mistakes?

4. Ask yourself, "Does the energy I am spending on self-loathing help anyone? If not, how might that energy be better directed?"

5. When you are successful in forgiving yourself, how does it happen?

6. To whom can you turn when self-talk doesn't do the job?

# CHAPTER 8

# THE ROLE OF APOLOGY

## How Apologies Heal

A good apology can foster healing but a faulty apology only makes a bad situation worse.

—Aaron Lazare

For people who have been harmed or who have committed a harm, an apology provides an important step on the path of forgiveness. In addition, an apology is an explicit strategy for repairing a relationship. When it is done well, an apology can promote healing for both the offender and the offended. It can begin to restore a sense of justice in the relationship and serve as a bridge to restore trust. While there's no guarantee that an apology will result in forgiveness, when it does, recovery from the damage committed can even regenerate relationships.

The ability to say *I'm sorry* at appropriate moments is a key skill in maintaining the health of your relationships. Saying the words *I'm sorry* can be difficult during times when you feel embarrassed by something you've done or shame for a wrong that you have committed. A genuine apology, spoken with compassion, can usually mitigate a bad situation. If your apology is accepted, you will have completed an important step on the path to forgiveness.

Kathryn Schultz, a researcher who studies how people react to their mistakes, argues that most of us will do anything to avoid admitting that we are wrong. However, Schultz points out,

The point isn't to live without any regrets ... the point is to not hate ourselves for having them.... We need to learn to love the flawed imperfect things that we create and to forgive ourselves for creating them. Regret doesn't remind us that we did badly; it reminds us that we know we can do better.[1]

## The Function of an Apology

Most people have internal rules about their relationships. When someone breaks one of these rules, an apology reaffirms the importance of both the rule and the relationship. An apology can also enable someone who has been harmed to save face, confirming his belief that the action was unfair. When you are harmed, an explanation and acceptance of responsibility by the transgressor can restore your trust in the one who committed the harm. If you want to continue the relationship, an apology signals your ongoing commitment to it. The apology can also serve as a peace offering to normalize the relationship.

Though simple phrases such as *I'm sorry* pass for an apology, the nature of apology is often more complicated than a single statement of remorse. In a review of research, Stanford psychologist Karina Schumann points out that apologies possess one or more of the following elements:

- Remorse: "I'm sorry."
- Acceptance of responsibility: "It's my fault."
- Admission of wrongdoing: "I shouldn't have done that."
- Acknowledgment of harm: "I know I hurt you."
- Explanation of reasons behind the harmful action: "I did this because I thought ..."
- A promise to behave better: "I will never do that again."
- A request for forgiveness: "Would you please forgive me?"
- An offer of restitution to repair the harm: "How can I repay you for what I've done?"[2]

When seeking forgiveness, your choice of wording depends on the significance of the relationship, the severity of the harm committed, and the context in which the harm occurred.

When Celia was in elementary school, she was overweight and had frizzy hair. One of her classmates, Jill, picked on her to a level we would characterize as bullying. However, Celia fought through her resentment and developed a resilience that served her well through her school years. Forty-five years later, when Celia returned to her hometown for a funeral, she met an old friend for coffee. In a moment of surprise, Jill, the same girl who had bullied Celia as a child, asked to join them. Jill said, "I hope I'm not interrupting, but I'd like to say something. I think back to our days in elementary school and I'm so sorry for things I said and did to you. I think the reason I was so mean is because my mother picked on me all the time."

Celia responded, "I forgave you years ago, because I didn't let it matter. Also, I understood that it wasn't about me; it was about you." In this case, when an apology came years later, Celia responded with grace and understanding. Celia's experience demonstrates most of the elements in Schumann's list of what is expected in an apology. Jill admitted doing wrong, demonstrated awareness that her behavior had caused Celia harm, expressed remorse for her actions, explained a little of the context behind the situation, and apologized for her behavior.

## Qualities of an Effective Apology

The effectiveness of an apology depends a great deal on the needs of the person who was harmed. For small offenses with few lasting consequences, *I'm sorry* may be sufficient. For example, suppose a teenager promises to take out the trash, but fails to do so. Her parents might view this responsibility as important at the moment, but by failing to follow through, she will not create lasting damage. However, with more serious offenses, such as causing a motor vehicle accident because you were driving under the influence of alcohol and injured a passenger, the victim may require you to sincerely acknowledge the harm, compensate him for losses he incurred, and demonstrate that you've changed your behavior. In this case, for the apology to be complete it must include specific information or explanations that the victim needs to hear.

In a genuine apology that sets the stage for forgiveness, you do the following:

- Acknowledge that an offense occurred.
- Accept responsibility for causing or contributing to the offense.

- Express remorse for the action.
- Make a commitment not to repeat the behavior.
- Offer to make reparations for the harm committed.

Even when all these elements are present, the person harmed might not easily accept the apology. Here are some additional factors that influence the outcome.

1. The way an apology is presented. Ideally, an apology should be made in person and include direct eye contact, showing warmth and sincerity. Eye contact should be direct but not aggressive. The transgressor's tone of voice should be calm and her body language should be inviting, with the offender turned toward the one she harmed with her arms relaxed. If the person harmed is making a judgment about the offender's sincerity or evaluating the intentions behind her apology, nonverbal messages must match the words. Humility needs to be linked to sincere empathy for the harms perpetrated. When an apology is offered, for the offended person, seeing is believing.

2. Intentions make a difference. When the person who has been harmed believes that the transgressor intended to do the harm, he is less willing to accept an apology.

3. Assess the health of the relationship before the offense. A person who is highly satisfied with a relationship tends to see greater sincerity in an apology, while a person with lower satisfaction tends to doubt the sincerity of an apology. Openness to an apology may also be influenced by personality traits, such as agreeableness, supportiveness, likability, openness, or warmth. In contrast, one researcher found that when a victim rated a relationship as less satisfying prior to a transgression, an apology didn't always result in forgiveness. In this case, the transgression might bring to the surface emotions connected to other problems in the relationship, complicating the acceptance of an apology.

4. Admit guilt or shame about a harm committed. Interestingly, the effect of expressing these emotions is not equal for men and women. It appears that women are more sensitive than men to expressions of sorrow and regret.

5. Consider the timing of an apology. If an apology is offered before both parties discuss the incident fully, it may be perceived as premature or insincere. This is especially true for more serious offenses. A central issue in timing is the need for the offended person to feel understood. This explains why a delayed apology might appear to be more satisfying than an early one. But how much delay is best? Researchers looked specifically at the issue of timing with romantic couples. They wanted to know how timing of an apology affected communication satisfaction, feeling understood, perception of sincerity, and the level of negative emotions. They found that with long-term conflicts allowing an issue to fester too long before discussing it may diminish the likelihood of forgiveness. A sincere apology reduced anger and irritation, but it did not immediately alleviate sadness or hurt. It appears these emotions take longer to dissipate.

6. Demonstrate respect. In harms that are perceived as unfair or unjust, an apology will be more graciously accepted if the offender demonstrates respect for the victim's feelings. This is important because respect conveys sincerity and genuineness, two qualities crucial to an effective apology.

| Effective Wording of an Apology | Why It Works |
|---|---|
| I'm sorry about what I said last night. | Takes responsibility for the behavior |
| I've been under a lot of pressure lately, but that's no excuse for my behavior. | Explains actions but does not excuse what has happened |
| I love you and will try harder not to say something like that again. | Promises to change behavior |
| I took what belonged to you. That was wrong. | Takes responsibility for the behavior |
| I apologize for my mistake. | Admits error |
| I shouldn't have done that. I'm returning your book. This will not happen again. | Promises no such hurtful behavior in the future |

| Ineffective Wording of an Apology | Why It Doesn't Work |
|---|---|
| I am sorry for whatever happened. | Vague language; offender fails to take responsibility |
| Mistakes were made. | Vague language; offender fails to take responsibility |
| I am sorry to the degree that you were hurt. | Minimizes the harm caused |
| Even the best of us makes mistakes. | Avoids responsibility and does not acknowledge specific harm |
| If I had known how you felt, I wouldn't have ... | Conditional apology, which shifts responsibility to the harmed person |
| I'm sorry that you misunderstood | Avoids responsibility; shifts blame to the offended person |

## Accepting an Apology

If someone offers you an apology, your first response is to evaluate whether she's expressing remorse, demonstrating sensitivity, and voicing an intention not to repeat the harm. If all these elements are present, your response would probably be "I forgive you." *New York Times* columnist David Brooks points out that even though we might hold on to doubts, "Trust doesn't have to be immediate but the wrong is no longer a barrier to the relationship."[3] When you accept an apology, it's important to be gracious and resist using the moment as an opportunity to get even.

Sometimes you may have doubts about aspects of the apology or you may not be emotionally ready to accept it. In these situations, it's appropriate to acknowledge that you are grateful for the apology, but you need time to work through some of your grief or disappointment. You might even ask if you can revisit the problem at a later time. You do not deny the apology or reject the person. Instead, you create space to evaluate the circumstances more freely and to ease your emotional response to what was done.

Another option when an apology is offered is to graciously accept it but, at the same time, ask questions to clarify things about the harm. For example,

"Can you help me understand what happened here?"

"Were you aware of how much this incident bothered me?"

"How can we prevent this from ever happening again?"

At this point, conversation becomes a moment of learning for both the offender and the offended.

## Why We're Unwilling to Apologize

Why is it so hard to say *I'm sorry*? For most people, saying these words requires a great deal of humility. Choosing to apologize also calls for the courage to accept the consequences of our actions. Psychologist Aaron Lazare explains that people often withhold apologies because they fear being rejected. In addition, saying *I'm sorry* may cause people to feel shame and guilt. According to Lazare,

> We are left with the paradox that the two major reasons for many people to apologize—changing the external world and relieving their inner feelings of guilt and shame—are the same reasons why others avoid apology—fearing the reaction of the external world and suffering from the emotions of guilt and shame.[4]

Sometimes your unwillingness to apologize may be related to having to swallow your pride. Because you want to appear strong and confident to those around you, admitting that you made a mistake undermines the positive image you want to project. It may be difficult to admit that you were wrong. However, admitting that you failed and expressing a desire to repair a problem in your relationship often constitute the strongest path. Many times in life, you are faced with two choices: a short uncomfortable time when you humble yourself and say, "I goofed. I'm sorry. Please forgive me," or a long uncomfortable time in which you live with tension in the relationship. Most people find that it's better to bring the problem to the surface and get over it than to let it fester and erode the relationship.

## When to Call on a Third Party

When you are emotionally upset, you may be unable to say things that would repair a bad situation. So, occasionally, it helps to request assistance from a third party. Because this third person is not emotionally involved in the situation, he or she might speak on your behalf and tell another that you are sorry for what happened or that fixing problems in your relationship is important to you. Third parties might include pastors who attempt to smooth out difficulties between congregants, a team member who conveys healing messages between workers who aren't getting along, or a family member who apologizes on behalf of another family member. The third party functions as a bridge to promote forgiveness and healing between parties who have difficulty talking to each other.

A person with a meaningful connection to both the offender and the offended can sometimes offer a third-party apology. Like any effective apology, it must contain a recognition of the injustice that was perpetrated, an expression of remorse, a commitment to change behavior, and a request for forgiveness.

It is not uncommon for heads of state to apologize for harmful actions committed by their countries decades or sometimes centuries earlier. For example, in 1995, U.S. ambassador Walter Mondale apologized to Japan on behalf of the United States for the U.S. bombing of Tokyo during World War II.[5] During the time she was secretary of state, Hillary Clinton apologized to the nation of Guatemala for research on seven hundred Guatemalan prisoners, between 1946 and 1948, involving sexually transmitted diseases. Clinton said, "Although these events occurred sixty-four years ago, we are outraged that such reprehensible research could have been conducted under the guise of public health. We deeply regret that it happened and apologize to all individuals who were affected."[6] Her apology acknowledged the wrong committed, accepted responsibility for it, and expressed remorse about the behavior.

> An apology is a lovely perfume; it can transform the clumsiest moment into a gracious gift.
>
> —MARGARET LEE RUNBECK

It is not uncommon for hospital directors to apologize for harmful actions committed by staff members, church officials to apologize for harmful actions by pastors or priests, and parents to apologize for harmful actions committed by their children. Julie, a survey participant, describes how she offered an apology on behalf of her husband, Phil, and Tim, her sixteen-year-old son, after Tim got into trouble at school. The teacher sent a strongly worded email to Phil, and he immediately sent a strongly worded email back, defending his son and telling the teacher to investigate all the facts before making accusations.

The teacher, also in a defensive posture, responded to the email with stronger words. Phil then sent an even stronger message back, accusing the teacher of being a bully, and he copied the message to the principal. Now, Julie became involved. She asked Phil to contact the teacher and explain the situation, but Phil refused. To fix what was escalating into a bad situation, Julie decided to meet with the teacher, explain the good intentions the father had in trying to protect his son, apologize for the email sent to the principal, and apologize for her son's behavior. As a calm third party, she could get beyond the heated emotions and promote a working relationship in the future.

## Helping Another Apologize

Not everyone accused of an offense will quickly choose to apologize. In these cases, a neutral third-party helper may meet separately with each of the parties to identify what needs to be done to resolve the situation amicably. If the person harmed believes an apology will help repair the relationship, the helper meets with the offender to determine his willingness to apologize. This third party may try to understand the intention behind the harmful act, the factors that led up to the act, and whether the offender feels remorse for the action. Inviting an offender to consider the perspective of the one harmed can be a helpful tactic in promoting forgiveness. It might even motivate the offender to apologize himself. The helper looks for a slightly open door that may promote the willingness to apologize. For example, the helper may ask,

"How would a person who has been harmed like this feel?"

"How would you feel if this happened to you?"

"Are you open to making this situation right?"

"Are you willing to give something a try to work through this problem?"

The third party may then help the offender craft a statement that can be shared with the one harmed. The statement will encompass many of the factors associated with effective apologies.

## When Apologies Fail

Researchers find that the value of an apology varies, depending on the situation. In some cases, the benefit of an apology may be overestimated. An apology does not necessarily alleviate the concerns of the harmed person; issues may still need to be addressed. Trust is not magically reborn when an offender says, "I'm sorry." Trust must be rebuilt through changed behavior. Restitution can address tangible losses, but intangible losses created by disappointment and heartbreak take time to repair.

An apology may fail for many reasons. Making excuses for bad behavior or blaming the victim may be perceived as failing to take responsibility for your actions. As mentioned earlier, if the offended person thinks that the offender meant to do her harm, she will be more reluctant to accept an apology as sincere or genuine.

Botched apologies almost always fail. For example, when California governor Arnold Schwarzenegger was accused of harassing women on his staff, he replied, "A lot of what you see in the stories is not true, but at the same time ... I have behaved badly sometimes ... I apologize because this is not what I tried to do."[7] He failed to directly acknowledge the wrong that he committed, failed to accept responsibility for his actions, and provided no assurance that he would change his behavior. When Senator Bob Packwood of Oregon was accused of harassing women, he said, "I'm apologizing for the conduct that it was alleged that I did."[8] His apology fails all the tests of an effective apology.

> There is no revenge so complete as forgiveness.
>
> —Josh Billings

Compare these two politicians' apologies with the public apology from professional golfer Tiger Woods following the revelation that he had many affairs while married to his wife, Elin:

> I want to say ... simply, and directly, I am deeply sorry for the irresponsible and selfish behavior I engaged in.... I am also aware of the pain my behavior has caused to those of you in this room. I have let you down ... I am so sorry. I have a lot to atone for ... It is now up to me to make amends. And that starts by never repeating the mistakes I have made. It is up to me to start living a life of integrity.[9]

Tiger Woods's statement demonstrates many of the elements of a successful apology. He takes responsibility for specific actions, demonstrates awareness of the emotional pain he caused others, and commits himself to atone for past actions and to engage in different behavior going forward.

Another type of botched apology involves minimizing or not acknowledging the damage that was done. In one example, a neighbor got tired of a little dog barking at her large dog. So to stop the little dog's barking, she let her big dog off its leash. The big dog attacked and almost killed her neighbor's little dog. When asked about the harm she committed, she said, "I'm sorry her little dog was hurt, but you know, I can't control all of my dog's actions. My neighbor should keep her little dog in the house." This type of apology fails because it is perceived as insincere and lacks compassion for those who were harmed. In most cases, people are looking for humility, remorse, and a commitment to repair the damage that was inflicted.

> The first to apologize is the bravest. The first to forgive is the strongest. And the first to forget is the happiest.
>
> —ANONYMOUS

Additionally, you can undermine the power of your apology if you are indirect and talk around the problem you are trying to resolve. Do your best to be direct and admit responsibility for what went wrong. Don't drag it out. The more explanation you provide, the greater the chance that you will resurrect the negative emotions and doubts you are trying to resolve. Be gracious and express concern about what the person you have harmed thinks and feels.

## Cultural Differences in Apologizing

Because culture influences how and what people communicate, it would make sense that the content and function of apology would differ across cultures. We know there are many differences between the style of apology commonly used in the United States and those used in other countries.

For example, in the United States, apologies often include an admission of guilt, acceptance of blame, and a statement of remorse. Sometimes they include an explanation, a clarification of expectations, and a commitment to changing behavior. In response to an apology, Americans tend to use more direct expressions, such as, "That's okay" or "I forgive you."

In Japan, those making apologies typically express remorse, but do not accept blame or responsibility. Instead, an apology tends to demonstrate understanding of the harm or burden created for the one offended. The apology will usually include few details. When Toyota drivers experienced problems with their accelerators, the CEO of Toyota issued a public apology, saying he was deeply sorry and described steps the company was taking to correct the problem, including what compensation for the problem would be offered. He did not admit fault, provide an explanation, or explain how this problem would be prevented in the future.

People of Chinese background typically use more facial expressions and fewer verbal statements to communicate their apologies. They also tend to use fewer conditional statements, such as "I will forgive you when I see ..." However, in both U.S. and Chinese cultures, an apology serves as a key predictor of forgiveness and relationship repair.

In any culture, apologies don't guarantee forgiveness. But they usually build a bridge that improves the likelihood of forgiveness. If the person making the apology is sincere, acknowledges and accepts responsibility for wrongdoing, and commits to changing his behavior, that contributes to the healing of the relationship. Forgiveness can occur without an apology, but it is a more difficult path and may leave unresolved emotions that surface later. When you offer an apology, you're saying, "I care and I want things to be different." It's the first step toward reconciliation in relationships.

## Questions

1. What's important for you to hear when you feel someone has said or done something that offended you?

2. When you have apologized to another, what did you want the other person to know?

3. When you received an apology from someone in the past, how did it affect the relationship?

4. There may be many ways to apologize without words, such as changing behavior, sharing a hug, or doing something kind for someone. What are some ways you apologize without using the words *I'm sorry*?

# CHAPTER 9

# RECONCILIATION

## THE BRIDGE TO REPAIRING A BROKEN RELATIONSHIP

> The journey toward reconciliation is not a path of the weak or feeble. Facing oneself and one's own fears and anxieties demands an outward and an inward journey.
>
> —John Paul Lederach

Dee and Jake lived in a small community in the Midwest. Together they had five children. When the youngest was in diapers and the eldest was ten years old, Dee announced, "I'm tired of all of this. I met someone in town and we are going to move to the West Coast." Then she left. Twenty years later, Dee returned to her hometown. She asked for forgiveness from her family and invited all of them to rebuild the relationships she had broken. Two of the grown children chose to forgive her but wanted no relationship with her. They had their own families now and had moved on from any need they might have had to establish a relationship with their mother.

Only one, the youngest son, reconciled with her. This son never married, had poor social skills, and his mother was all that he had. He told her that he would take care of her. The two other children who wouldn't forgive or reconcile with their mother chose to treat her with indifference, refusing to see her or talk to her. In this family, forgiveness did not mean reconciliation.

There is a great deal of agreement among both theologians and psychologists that, at a minimum, forgiveness involves letting go of negative feelings and replacing them with goodwill toward others. However, little

consensus exists as to whether forgiveness should always lead to reconciliation. In some settings, reconciliation may not be healthy for the one
harmed, while, in others, it may be the only path to healing old wounds.
Once again, the severity of the offense and the significance of the harm
have a great deal to do with whether reconciliation is appropriate or even
desired.

## What Is Reconciliation?

Forgiveness will usually help people get over negative thinking and
unhealthy emotions caused by past harms. At the same time, you can forgive another without choosing to resume the relationship. However, if you
want to repair the relationship, the process of reconciliation, like that of
forgiveness, may require hard work and sustained commitment.

Psychologist Everett Worthington characterizes reconciliation as a bridge
between two parties, each one standing their ground with a divide between
them. Bridging the divide involves five phases:

1. Decide if, how, what, and when to reconcile
2. Discuss the harms that were committed
3. Detoxify the relationship from past hurts
4. Mutually commit to repairing the relationship
5. Devote time and energy to reconciliation efforts[1]

In attempting reconciliation, it's especially important to curb destructive
communication cycles that sometimes take hold in relationships. Oftentimes, these reflect patterns of attacking and defending. Common statements in these kinds of cycles include:

> "You disappoint me."
> "If you hadn't done that, this wouldn't have happened."
> "I don't think you're capable of getting it right."
> "Nothing is good enough for you. I did my best."

Getting past these patterns may call for a truce in which both parties agree
to stop saying and doing things that purposely aggravate the other. It may
mean refraining from making critical statements about the other, as well
as stopping annoying behaviors, such as interrupting the other person or

rolling eyes after the other one talks. These toxic behaviors usually get in the way of both forgiveness and reconciliation.

Although Worthington's phases of reconciliation do not predict success, they may create favorable dynamics through the release of hurt or anger. In most cases, genuine forgiveness must precede reconciliation. Otherwise, remnants of resentment or lack of trust can sabotage any attempts to repair the relationship. Psychologist Robert Enright points out that reconciliation cannot begin until negative emotions subside.[2] The timing for emotions to diminish can be anywhere from days to years.

## Unintentional versus Intentional Reconciliation

Unintentional reconciliation differs significantly from intentional reconciliation. When parties say little as they wait for things to change or the other person to take the lead, that constitutes unintentional reconciliation. The offender makes no apology, offers no assurances, promises no behavior change in the future, and initiates no discussion of harms that have been committed. In spite of this, victims will sometimes heal with no conversation about the issue, just with the passage of time. This can be a risky strategy, however, because it allows resentment to grow. The danger in this approach is that there may come a point of no return, where the hurt from the offense is too deep to repair.

> The overall purpose of human communication is—or should be—reconciliation.
>
> —M. Scott Peck

By contrast, intentional reconciliation involves taking the risk to bring the divisive issues to the surface. Both parties attempt to authentically discuss the extent of the harm done and what steps may be needed to repair the situation. Completing these steps requires a safe climate in which to hold the discussion as well as a commitment by all parties to working on the problem. If these things are in place, you'll have a good chance of repairing the relationship.

When you are intentionally seeking reconciliation, these guidelines will help you achieve your goal:

1. Choose a time and a place where there will be few distractions.
2. Focus on the problem, not each other.
3. Listen to understand, not to argue.

4. Ask for clarification of what is unclear.

5. Problem-solve before deciding on solutions.

6. Build on learning from the past, rather than being consumed by the past.

Intentional reconciliation is often linked to the concept of making peace with an adversary. When forgiveness precedes reconciliation, adversaries agree to cease hostility, suspend thinking about revenge, and limit negative thoughts about the other. Communication shifts from emotionally harmful words to words that are neutral or positive. To achieve reconciliation, the parties don't have to like each other, but they must be civil to one another. If communication swings back into negative territory, the parties need to rewind the conversation to a point of greater tolerance and pick up from there. The goal of reconciliation is to create conditions in which both parties can live without fear of harm recurring. Based on the needs of a relationship, you might see any of these possibilities:

| 1<br>No forgiveness<br>No reconciliation | 3<br>Forgiveness<br>No reconciliation |
|---|---|
| 2<br>Reconciliation<br>No forgiveness | 4<br>Reconciliation<br>Forgiveness |

In the case of Dee, who abandoned her husband and family, most of her children favored the first of these options. Only the youngest son chose option 2, to reconcile with his mother but without offering her forgiveness

## Partial Reconciliation versus Full Reconciliation

Sometimes reconciliation happens but only at one level. In this case, partial reconciliation may require you to live without the transgressor making changes in patterns of behavior or thinking and not dealing with the roots of the harm done. When you engage in partial reconciliation, you may decide to hide your true feelings and withhold resentment to get along with the one who harmed you. For the sake of continuing to live or work together in peace, you may agree to move on without resolving the divide in the relationship. Unfortunately, this type of forgiveness is shallow and incomplete. You might ignore the harm in hope that the other person's memory will fade over time or that the problem will go away without saying anything. While this appears to bring reconciliation, it may create an unstable truce with resentments that can overshadow your relationship.

An example of partial reconciliation occurred between Kim and Shirley, the managers of two departments who had worked together reasonably well for eight years. Their communication broke down after Shirley began complaining to their boss, a vice president, about the way Kim managed her staff. Hearing about Shirley's complaint, Kim told this same vice president that Shirley was a gossip, frequently undermining the work of Kim's staff. The problem burst out into the open when no one on Kim's staff attended the company holiday party that had been planned by Shirley's staff.

When work on shared projects began to break down between Kim's and Shirley's departments, the vice president said, "That's enough." He called the two employees together and demanded that they both forgive and forget. They both agreed and, on the surface, it appeared that the vice president's admonition had worked. The two spoke congenially at meetings and encouraged their staffs to cooperate with each other. However, after a few months, the two began sitting at opposite ends of the table during company meetings and they stopped talking to each other. Kim and Shirley demonstrated partial reconciliation. They agreed to forgive and reconcile, but the agreement was superficial and their forgiveness was shallow. In order to bring about an effective interdepartmental collaboration, they needed to work through their unresolved issues, with the goal of forging a stable, authentic reconciliation.

To achieve full reconciliation, both the offender and the offended must accept responsibility for their part in harms committed. For example, a manager who writes up an employee may have to admit to not providing the best direction for getting tasks accomplished. The employee may have to accept responsibility for complaining about the manager or not following through on tasks, just to irritate the manager. Full reconciliation requires commitment to mutual healing and to preventing similar harms from recurring.

For full reconciliation to occur, both parties must identify and satisfy the needs of the other. Consider a family in which a widow had three grown daughters and a grown son, Henry. Henry lived a considerable distance from the rest of his family. When Henry's father died, he left a provision in his will that his family had to reach consensus on the distribution of his estate before any of them received anything. Unfortunately, the family went many years without achieving consensus, so the inheritance sat unclaimed. Eventually, the family went to a mediator. In the negotiations, the mediator found that the son was the primary stumbling block to reaching an agreement. In a private session the mediator asked Henry, "What gives?" Henry replied, "We cannot settle this matter until I receive an apology about the glove." He explained that one day when he was a young boy on his way to school in the winter, his sisters took his glove and played keep-away with it. They laughed at him and teased him.

> I can forgive, but I cannot forget, is only another way of saying, I will not forgive. Forgiveness ought to be like a cancelled note—torn in two, and burned up, so that it never can be shown against one.
>
> —HENRY WARD BEECHER

He could never forget that humiliating day. Back in session, the mediator asked the family if the sisters were ready to help Henry with these feelings. Together, the sisters exclaimed, "Oh, Henry was such a sissy. He still is. He just has to get over it!" The family left that day without a settlement. Until they address Henry's need to feel valued and respected, they will reach no agreement about this inheritance and no reconciliation.

This example demonstrates that reconciliation is unlikely to occur until Henry's needs are addressed. If Henry can forgive his sisters for their critical attitude toward him, it could be the first step toward forgiveness. This forgiveness may also call for words of understanding from the sisters or empathy for Henry's emotional distress. To restore the relationship, the siblings will need to make a firm commitment to value and respect one another. In addition, reconciliation may require an apology and new behavior that displays a change of attitude. Because the patterns established by this family date back many years, a great deal of hard work will be required for them to rebuild trust and commitment.

Writer Laura Davis explains the moment when reconciliation is complete:

> When I have deep reconciliation, I can always tell because I have
> no interest in talking about the problem anymore. When some-
> thing feels unresolved, I feel like a dog with a bone. I keep return-
> ing to it and gnawing at it. But when something is really taken care
> of, the problem loses its charge, and I lose interest; I don't want to
> stir the pot anymore.[3]

## The Role of Repentance

For some people, an offender's *I'm sorry* is not enough to justify reconciliation. In these cases, reconciliation requires repentance on the part of
the transgressor, and a visible change of behavior that justifies renewed
trust in the offender. Repentance means that the offender acknowledges
that a wrong has been done, assumes responsibility for that wrong, and
commits to doing things differently now and in the future. Repentance
enables the one harmed to see the offender's genuine commitment to the
relationship and to behavior that will prevent a recurrence of the undesirable behavior. Crucial elements for repentance include:

1. Remorse: Admission of wrongdoing
2. Responsibility: Acceptance of one's contribution to the harms
   committed
3. Apology: Asking for forgiveness
4. Restitution: Giving back what was taken
5. Lessons learned: Addressing the character flaws that caused the
   offense

Remember Dee, the woman who left her family and didn't return for
twenty years? In spite of her apology, she failed the test on all five factors of repentance. Her children rejected her apology because she took an
important relationship away from them—that of their relationship with
their mother—during their formative years.

Remorse, apology, forgiveness, repentance, and reconciliation are all inter-
twined, much like strands of a rope. Each of these factors supports the others.
Remorse and apology aid the work of forgiveness while repentance demonstrates remorse and a change of heart. Each step of reconciliation builds on

the commitment made in the apology and the response of forgiveness. When one of these factors begins to fail, reconciliation may unravel.

## Rewriting the Story

One tactic that can help people achieve reconciliation is to develop a new story about past incidents. If you continue to review unpleasant details of a past harm and keep feeling victimized and helpless, it may be difficult to achieve reconciliation. Creating a new narrative reframes a past event and replaces the negative elements with more positive ones. Rather than focusing on someone's failure, the parties involved look at what was learned from the experience. Patti, a survey participant, told us about her sad childhood in which she moved between numerous foster families. Instead of talking about the tragedy of her childhood, she created a story of success as a result of the trials she endured and how this helped her learn adaptability. She described her long, happy marriage and how she came to appreciate someone who loved her.

> The practice of peace and reconciliation is one of the most vital and artistic of human actions.
>
> —THICH NHAT HANH

In transforming their stories, each of the parties expresses him- or herself without attacking the other. Each person also takes two risks. The first risk is to identify and speak about the pain that you carry inside. The second risk involves a willingness to listen with interest and empathy to those who share their own pain. You have to be willing to walk alongside others on their journeys. If you approach the words of another with defensiveness or argument, the transforming process will be shut down.

Ruth had not spoken to her younger sister, Emily, in many years. This rift started when Ruth's seven-year-old daughter died of congenital heart failure. During the pre-funeral gathering at Ruth's home, Emily was overcome with grief about losing her niece and fell to the floor, sobbing hysterically. The large number of guests and family members were horrified by Emily's behavior, but didn't know how to respond. After the funeral was over, Ruth pulled Emily aside and said, "Did you have to make such a horrible display? This was my day to remember my daughter. This is not about you." Emily became angry and replied, "You're not honoring my feelings," and she stomped out of the room. Ruth tried to stay in touch with her sister with phone messages and cards, but Emily would not respond. Neither forgiveness nor reconciliation appeared possible.

Then a transformative event occurred. Emily's daughter set her wedding date and planned a reception and dance. Ruth decided to go to her niece's wedding but avoid her sister by forgoing the dance. However, her niece convinced Ruth that she needed her to be at the wedding dance for just a while. So Ruth agreed to attend. During the first moments of the dance, her niece arranged all the "important women in her life" in a circle while music played. During an impromptu group dance, Ruth and Emily, who had been placed next to each other, bumped into each other and fell into each other's arms. As they held each other, they both began to cry.

> Compassion, forgiveness, these are real, ultimate sources of power for peace and success in life.
>
> —DALAI LAMA

They hugged each other and began a conversation with *I'm sorry we've been apart.* A spontaneous dialogue began that continued well into the evening. Their stories, in which they blamed each other for the estrangement, were transformed into how they had let each other down, and they created a new story of healing for the relationship and the family.

## Where to Begin

If you decide to work toward reconciliation, we propose that you consider the following process.

- Select the best way to reach out. This depends a great deal on the nature of the problem, the length of time it has gone on, and the method in which you feel safest. You might choose to reach out in person, on the phone, in a letter, or in an email. If you decide to meet in person, choreograph the time and setting for maximum effect, both for yourself and for the one with whom you are repairing the relationship.

- Before you approach the person, identify the issues you want to talk about. Begin with the easiest ones first. Before sending a letter or an email, let a friend read it to check for unhelpful tones. If you are going to meet in person, rehearse what you plan to say with a friend. Remember that emotion tends to distort the meaning of our words, so become conscious of what you are feeling and do your best to manage it. Be prepared for how you will respond if the other person becomes defensive, attempts to make you feel guilty, or verbally attacks you. If you respond to attacking statements with counterattacks, the negative cycle continues; this may further harm the relationship. Instead, take a gentle, positive approach. If you are a spiritual person, pray for the right words that will repair what is broken.

- Be prepared to share how you have been harmed as well. Even if you were the offender, you can speak of the alienation that has occurred, the loss of a relationship that you valued, how much you have missed this person, or the feelings of shame about what you did.

- Move slowly and speak carefully. When you speak quickly to "get something off your chest," you raise the risk of being misunderstood, saying something you don't mean, or allowing your emotions to overwhelm your thinking. You want to avoid having the other person jump to conclusions or become defensive. Speak carefully, editing out the words that might trigger additional hurt.

- As much as possible, deal with one problem at a time. Focus on an understanding of what led to the problem and, instead of assigning blame, note the effect it had on each of you. Try to picture yourself approaching the other person with an open hand, rather than a clenched fist.

- Be careful about generating solutions too quickly. Take time to understand what led to the problem and the effect it had on each of you. Moving too quickly runs the risk of pushing the other person further away.

- If reconciliation occurs, discuss how you will both work to prevent a relationship breakdown in the future. Talk about what you want the relationship to become and conclude with a ritual of a toast, a hug, or plans for another meeting.

## Factors That Promote Reconciliation

The benefits and the value of the relationship will play pivotal roles in your decision as to whether you commit to reconciliation. Much of this will be related to your level of past satisfaction in the relationship. If the harm stemmed from a job in which a manager offended you, you would compare the stress of changing jobs with your level of satisfaction in your current job. If you have been betrayed by a partner or a spouse, you would compare the cost of giving up the current relationship with having no relationship at all. This evaluation may be complicated if you have children, joint finances, and shared property. In both these cases, anticipated future rewards can serve as a basis for deciding how much additional investment you want to make in the relationship.

The willingness of a victim to give people the benefit of the doubt will also affect reconciliation. Attributing the problem to some outside source, such as job stress, improves the chance that the offended person will offer forgiveness. Social psychologist Eli Finkel and colleagues explain that if the victim can put a positive spin on details of the infraction or accept some small responsibility for the events that occurred, the odds go up for repairing the relationship.[4]

Empathy and understanding act as important steps on a bridge to reconciliation. When you believe that the transgressor understands how you feel, you may see more hope for the situation. Empathy on the part of the offender demonstrates that he cares about the relationship as well as the person he has harmed. It can also promote a willingness to reciprocate: "Because you demonstrated caring for me, I will do the same for you." Though sometimes difficult to endure, conflict can provide an opportunity for a relationship to grow stronger. By working through the conflict, each of the parties gains a better understanding of the other.

People need to reestablish trust before reconciliation can be achieved. To accomplish this, you will need to focus on the welfare and feelings of the other person. Initially, your displays of caring may be met with resistance, but over time consistent messages of concern build a connection. The restoration of trust may come slowly. This is because trust involves many factors, including:

- Expecting another to act in beneficial ways
- Belief that another will sacrifice her personal need for the needs of the relationship
- Confidence in positive outcomes
- Respect for agreed-upon norms established for the relationship

- Safeguards built into the relationship to protect the parties from harm
- Responsiveness to an expressed need

Investing in the future of the relationship also plays a significant role in reconciliation. In a study of thirty-six couples, researchers Bruce Patterson and Dan O'Hair found a common element for those who were successful in reconciling past problems.[5] Virtually all the couples took time out to evaluate their goals for the future of the relationship. Each person gave his or her partner permission not to talk about their relationship problems for a short time to give each other some space away from the harmful communication in the relationship. When discussion resumed, couples focused on sharing their needs in open, honest conversation. Reconciliation requires a commitment of time, quality communication, and the determination to devote energy to the relationship. In addition, addressing how you talk about issues can promote more constructive management of tension. For example, you can offer such comments as the following:

- I think I'm missing your point. Please tell me what you think again.
- I notice how the volume is increasing. Perhaps we could both tone it down a little and listen a little harder to what each other is saying.
- It looks like we're both after the same thing. How can we work together to achieve it?
- I think we're getting away from the issue that concerns us both. Can we return to the question we began with?

You also need to make it clear that both of you are in this together and you need to solve problems together. Though you might be inclined to be defensive, make sure you strive to be open and flexible as you try to understand the issues that divide you.

## Factors That Prevent Reconciliation

In the realm of human relationships, there are probably more reasons not to reconcile than good reasons to reconcile. A partner who has suffered harm argues, "I will not allow this to happen to me again." Some say, "That person must suffer just as much as I have." It is also common to hear a partner express resignation: "I just don't feel like trying anymore." Attempting to repair a relationship requires new risks of vulnerability. You may have to bring up issues that you would just as soon forget, or make efforts to communicate when you are tired or depressed. Whether you have been harmed or have harmed another, your thought patterns can become rigid and stubborn, as you erect barriers to resolving differences. Reconciliation will require a softening of these attitudes in order to make progress.

As we pointed out earlier, destructive communication cycles may make your relationship so toxic that efforts to restore the relationship may not be possible. Hurtful comments create attack-and-defend responses. These destructive cycles sabotage efforts to heal old wounds. They also undermine trust and may erode the willingness to forgive. One of you needs to break the cycle by defusing the situation and demonstrating an interest in trying to understand what the real issues are and address them.

Barriers to reconciliation are sometimes a function of personality problems. For example, someone who is emotionally unexpressive may be unable to provide the emotional support requested by her partner. Someone with a disagreeable attitude may come across as stubborn or unwilling to cooperate. A person with a self-centered personality may seem unwilling to recognize and value the needs of others. The drive for reconciliation may require some people to undergo psychological change and healing before they can repair their relationships.

Diane and Rob got married a year out of high school. Rob wanted to start his own business and Diane wanted to go to college. Their dreams were interrupted by three children born over the next six years. During this time, their relationship became punctuated with destructive emotional dramas and times when they didn't speak to each other for weeks on end. Both were emotionally immature and emotionally unhealthy. After twenty years of marriage, Diane left the home, announcing, "It's over." For the next seven years, after her divorce from Rob, she reinvented herself through singles groups and community service activities. She worked on her self-esteem, her communication skills, and her self-confidence. She married a wonderful man and developed a healthy relationship with him. When she returned to her hometown, she discovered that Rob had undergone similar changes. Together they attended their children's weddings and were there for the birth of their grandchildren. Though they had moved on to new relationships, both freely admitted,

"If we had met each other now, we would have an entirely different marriage." But they could not reach this point of reconciliation until they each became psychologically healthier.

## The Blessing of Reconciliation

The importance of reconciliation is captured in the biblical story of two brothers who became estranged. The younger brother, Jacob, had tricked his father into giving him the family inheritance. The older brother, Esau, was furious and left the family. He was gone for twenty years. When Jacob heard about Esau's plan to return home, his fear was represented in a dream about wrestling with angels. Fearing for his life, Jacob prayed, "Deliver me, please, from the hand of my brother ... for I am afraid of him; he may come and kill us all" (Genesis 22:11).

> Put away from you all bitterness and wrath and anger and wrangling and slander, together with all malice, and be kind to one another, tenderhearted, forgiving one another, just as God in Christ has forgiven you.
>
> —EPHESIANS 4:31–31, NRSV

Esau, however, had forgiven his brother for his behavior long before he came home. Upon seeing Jacob, Esau ran across a field to hug him and reestablish the relationship that he had lost. Here's the point of this story: reconciliation may call for mercy and forgiveness as a first step to restoring a relationship.

## Questions

1. If you are the victim of someone else's harmful actions, what is your response?

2. In your life, how has forgiveness been related to reconciliation?

3. When you were a child, how did the adults in your life model reconciliation? Did people just hope bad behavior would be forgotten or did they openly discuss the behavior?

4. What are some situations where you could forgive but not choose reconciliation?

5. Where in your life do you need to experience reconciliation? What would it take to get that process started?

# CHAPTER 10

# WHEN FORGIVING AND RECONCILING ARE DIFFICULT

## OVERCOMING THE FACTORS THAT PREVENT FORGIVENESS

*The mind creates the abyss and the heart crosses it.*

—Nisargadettta Maharaj, Jnana Yoga Master

Insensitive behaviors in relationships create heartaches that may be felt for a long time. We each need to feel appreciated, valued, and loved, so when someone says or does something that harms us, it can be difficult to get over it. For example, a middle-aged man talks about the destructive behaviors he endured in the past and why he's unwilling to forgive his mother: "When I was a young boy and throughout my childhood, my mother was always angry at me, telling me that I was doing things wrong. She routinely complained that all I ever did was break her heart. Eventually, I behaved in ways that proved to her that I was as bad as she said I was." This man and his mother lived in a cycle of verbal abuse, both accused of failing the other. Memories like these shadow the emotional lives of many adults. Unless you have new positive experiences to counter them, these early issues can keep you from having healthy relationships. They undermine your confidence and harm your self-esteem. Identifying why you won't let go of a painful memory or why you can't forgive might provide the first step in healing a relationship.

Many factors may explain why you may not be able to let go of negative emotions from your past. Some of the most common ones include these:

- Relationship history
- Loss and coping with it
- History of self-repair
- Inner drama
- Lingering resentment[1]

## Relationship History: Our Past Affects Our Present

In your early years, you develop patterns of closeness or distance when it comes to your friends and family members. If you've grown to expect that people won't love you, you carry that into your teen and adult relationships. In the same way, if your life experiences teach you that people will disappoint you and not be there when you need them, you might carry that expectation over into adult relationships. Without psychological or spiritual repair, you may live with unsatisfied emotional and relationship needs. We can grieve the loss of what we didn't have. You can grieve a mother's love that you didn't receive, a father's support that wasn't there, or the friendship of a sibling who never cared for you. Learning to connect to others in a healthy, emotionally satisfying manner is one of the most important tasks of our development. For some people, emotional memories of unsatisfying past relationships cast a shadow over relationships throughout life. Being able to forgive people from your past can help you improve your relationships.

> Do not let the sun go down on your anger.
>
> —EPHESIANS 4:26, NRSV

As a young girl, Joyce lived with her parents, two younger sisters, and a brother. She had a very poor relationship with her mother, and describes her mother as always scolding her, rarely appreciating her, and never once saying she loved her. In spite of her best efforts, Joyce never figured out how to please her mother or earn the love and respect her two sisters received. When Joyce was ten, she told her mother about a recent family visit to her uncle's home. During that visit, while others were out, her uncle sexually assaulted her. Her mother discounted Joyce's story and told her never to bring it up again. After this, Joyce's relationship with her mother went further downhill. As an adult, Joyce continued to try to earn her mother's love by visiting her, calling once in a while, and sending cards throughout the year, but never felt her mother's love or appreciation. Joyce was particularly hurt when her sister let it slip that the other two sisters and her mom were planning a trip to visit relatives and Joyce had not been invited. Once again, she felt rejected. Joyce's history with her mother undermined her emotional well-being. In this situation, Joyce may be able to forgive her mother, but reconciliation would be especially challenging.

The good news is that forgiveness can help you ease anxiety you feel about your past. You are not trapped by your past. As you forgive those who have disappointed or harmed you, you can let go of those memories and focus on the present. In your current relationships, you can give and expect appreciation, compassionate caring, and love without comparing them to relationships of the past. Perhaps your new mantra can become, "It doesn't have to be that way now. I will do things differently."

## Coping with Loss: Not Letting Our Losses Determine Our Future

People who have experienced a great deal of loss carry the scars from these times through life. Loss of a job, a broken relationship, or a death of or alienation from a parent all become sources of anxiety that can cloud the present. In some cases, the disappointments may be small, such as a friend forgetting to return a call, being gossiped about at work, or being yelled at by someone you care about. In adult life, struggling with these past negative emotions contributes to setbacks you experience through life.

Grieving your losses may be self-consuming. You become preoccupied with "poor me" thinking. Unfortunately, focusing on the past distracts you from devoting your full attention to the present. Grieving what you didn't get instead of what you do have points you backward and promotes an attitude of helplessness.

Barbara is a sixty-year-old woman who grew up with an alcoholic and abusive father. Because of this, Barbara relied heavily on her mother's support, which wasn't always there. For her first fifty years, Barbara forgave her mother, understanding the difficult life her mother led. But for the past ten years, Barbara could no longer accept her mother's excuses for letting her down at times when it counted. On a recent weekend, Barbara planned a Sunday birthday party for her six-year-old grand-daughter and invited her mother. On Saturday afternoon, Barbara's mother called and said, "I'm sorry, but I may be late or not get to the party because my cousin Louie died. I'm going to the funeral at noon on Sunday." Barbara was upset. She said, "Once again, my mother has let me down. She barely knows this cousin and yet his funeral takes prior-ity over an important event in my granddaughter's life." The loss that Barbara is feeling may have less to do with this birthday party and more to do with fifty years of unresolved emotion about her mother's lack of support.

To alter the patterns associated with disappointment and loss, you need to invest in three areas of your life: happiness, connection, and meaning. When you are low in any one of these dimensions, you open yourself up to reliving the wounds of the past.

> **Happiness.** Doing activities that strengthen your emotional core, so that the wounds of the past consume a smaller propor-tion of your thinking and feeling.
>
> **Connection.** Creating new attachments with healthy people—people who will value you, support you, and accept you as you are.
>
> **Meaning.** Devoting energy to connecting with your inner spirit, such as developing skills of contemplation or prayer, or nur-turing your mind by reading a book that thoroughly engrosses you. You might try playing music to exercise the creative part of your brain, or enjoying the day by walking in the sunshine or going to a park.

When it comes to letting go of emotions, research suggests that women hold on to sadness longer, but men cling to anger longer.[2] For example, Walter tells us that fifteen years ago his marriage broke apart. He blamed his wife for having an affair and he blamed himself for working many weeks out of town. A few years ago, his wife remarried, but, because of their grown children, they still occasionally see each other. He laments, "I'm still angry and I'm still disappointed. I would marry her again today if I had the chance. I just can't let it go."

Because Walter will not let go of his anger, forgiveness and reconciliation are difficult. He recognizes that he holds on to his feelings to keep from seeing himself as weak or as a victim. He has difficulty admitting that he lacks control over the situation. At the same time, letting go means accepting that the relationship is finally over. For Walter to let go of his anger, he needs to be willing to do several things:

- Move on emotionally. He needs to let it go.
- Accept that the world isn't perfect. He still believes that "Things like this should never happen."
- Face his emptiness. If he lets go of his anger, he has nothing. There is a hole inside him that has not been filled.
- Do the work it takes to get over his anger. He feels that this will be too hard.

## Our History of Self-Repair: Taking Better Care of Ourselves

As a child, you begin a process of learning how to take care of yourself. You learn how to respond to disappointment, how to bounce back from the words of an angry playmate—"You can't play with us," "We don't like you"—and how to regain your confidence after you've failed at something. You begin to understand that some problems are not about you, but about someone else's unhappiness. You learn resilience, the ability to take care of yourself in spite of obstacles you encounter in the world around you. When you encounter similar disappointments or harm as an adult, your ability to respond graciously with mercy and forgiveness is a reflection of your having learned to adapt, cope, and manage your emotions.

> Good-nature and good-sense must ever join; To err is human, to forgive, divine.
>
> —ALEXANDER POPE

Some people grow up with a poor history of self-repair. They may have had weak adult modeling or parents who made most decisions for them. They lacked experience dealing with frustration or loss. One mother told us how her son, as a young child, lied and stole from others. To protect him she bailed him out of every problem she could. As an adult, he has struggled with a lot of life issues. Instead of taking responsibility for his actions, he blames the court system for not being more forgiving, his girl-friend for not taking care of him, and his employers for not being patient with him when he skips work. His inability to manage himself in relation to life's challenges is a direct reflection of how unskilled he became at self-repair as he grew up.

Norman Doidge, a medical doctor, characterizes the brain as a ski slope with a familiar pattern of tracks that have been created over time.[3] Just like a ski slope, your brain develops mental tracks that reflect par-ticular ways of thinking. If you spend years being told that you can't do something, you begin to believe it and create a mental image of how helpless you are. If you believe that you are incapable of healthy relation-ships, you may fall into recurring patterns that undermine your relation-ships. Self-repair may call for you to create new self-messages and alter these old patterns. You might need to engage in uncomfortable activities, such as talking with someone you haven't spoken to in a long time. You might have to step out of your comfort zone and forge a new pattern of thinking or behavior.

## Inner Drama: Changing the Story We Tell

We grow up in families that can be described as comedies, tragedies, adventures, or mysteries. The kind of family drama you experienced as a child has a great deal to do with the dramas you reproduce in life as an adult. Jenny, a graduate student who was one of our survey participants, said, "My family was always frustrated and angry about something. Every day was an emotional drama. Unfortunately, I see the same dynamics in my own family today. My sons and daughters come to me with problems that seem like such big emotional dramas." Similarly, Chuck, an older man, said, "My family was a source of continuous chaos. I still feel the lingering effects of that chaos within me." At work, Chuck was the predict-able cynic when it came to new ideas. At home, he was the pessimist who criticized his wife's plans. At the core of his personal drama was the belief that "Life will disappoint you sooner or later." The drama of your inner life is often a reflection of the dramas you learned in early childhood or in relationships you had in life.

People whose inner dramas are unsatisfying may find themselves creat-ing similar ongoing dramas through life. Betty, an elderly woman who had trouble talking to her daughter without getting into an argument, confessed, "My life has always been that way. I had two sisters and we argued incessantly. In each of my marriages, we fought and argued. And I don't know how to talk to my daughter without creating that same emotional drama."

You might be slow to forgive or reconcile because your internal drama is filled with stress, and you can't picture life without it. But not everyone lives this way. Some people have internal dramas that show them handling any problem that comes their way with ease. They might also see themselves as people who promote harmony and peace in their relationships. You have the choice of two paths in your relationships:

> **Path 1:** Your personal internal drama pictures you as preoccupied with past loss or disappointment, trapped in unhealthy relationships that you feel unable to repair, or engaged in unhealthy patterns that leave you doubting yourself.
>
> **Path 2:** Your personal internal drama pictures you in healthy relationships; your role is one of a peacemaker and harmonizer, who adapts well to change and who forgives easily.

To move from the first path to the second path you must take risks to change the script. You need to accept that life doesn't have to be as it has been. This means forgiving those who have harmed you in the past, forgiving yourself, and forgiving others for letting you down. The process begins with taking charge of your life. You can choose to surround yourself with people who treat you with respect, grace, and appreciation. You can also choose to let go of negative dramas from the past and develop a new drama in which you live successfully and peacefully.

## Lingering Resentment: Fixed on the Past

If you can't let go of emotional memories, you might have a need to hold on to resentment. In that case, you just don't want to let go. Unfortunately, resentment is destructive. It preoccupies your thinking, causes you to dwell on negative thoughts, and drains you of energy. This is especially true in broken relationships. "He must suffer as I suffered" or "She needs to feel the loss I've felt"—these emotions are linked to a need for justice or revenge. They are also linked to a lack of satisfying closure for a relationship.

When Ron came to see his counselor, he spoke of his sadness and depression related to a broken marriage. He said, "She hurt me so much and I just can't get over it. I miss her, but I hope she's miserable in her new relationship." When asked how long it has been since the relationship ended, Ron said, "Ten years." Ron's sorrow continues to fuel his resentment toward his former wife. His inability to forgive and move on hurts him more than it harms her. As difficult as it is, Ron would improve his emotional state by doing the opposite of what he feels: wishing his former wife happiness.

To overcome the emotional memories connected with a need for justice, create new self-messages that counter the negative emotions:

- It's a waste of time and energy to fight what already occurred.
- Wishing harm to a former friend will not help me now.
- I've had enough time to heal; it's time to get on with life.
- I made some decisions that didn't serve me well. I would make different decisions now.
- I can be whole and strong again, in spite of what happened to me. I will make it so.

## Living with Grace: Separating the Past from the Present

Living with grace is an attitude that is central to the concept of forgiveness. Grace allows you to extend compassion, acceptance, and forgiveness to others, whether they deserve it or not. Many of life's experiences may predispose you to doubt yourself and make harsh judgments of others. You may hold yourself and others accountable for old rules about what should be done and how things should be. These rules can undermine your self-confidence or your willingness to develop good relationships with others. Living with grace involves separating past bad memories from the needs of the present. You recognize that your current situation is different from the past. You remind yourself that the person you are relating to is different from someone who let you down in the past. Grace is accepting people as they are and beginning with positive expectations, rather than negative ones. Three principles that might help us to live with more grace are these:

1. Give yourself permission to make mistakes. Our lives are so busy that it's difficult to get it all right. You beat yourself up when you make mistakes. Perhaps you think you can be everything to everyone, which simply wears you out. This also breeds self-doubt and damages your relationships along the way. Living with grace means giving yourself and others permission to make mistakes. It also leaves room for you to grow and learn from your failures.

2. Coach yourself with self-talk. Some possibilities of the kinds of things you might say to yourself include:

   • This is not the person I am really angry at.

   • This time I'm going to manage this kind of situation better than I did in the past.

   • It may take some practice, but I will get through this.

   • I won't say much until I calm down a little.

   • Though I feel anxious, I will smile and say something positive.

   • I can ask questions until I figure out what is going on inside me.

3. Update your expectations. Many of your expectations of life were built before you were an adult. Relax expectations that were too high and wore you out. Allow yourself the grace to change your plans, set new goals, and approach life's journey with more flexibility.

## The Harm of a Rigid Outlook

Forgiveness can be difficult if you have rigid expectations that leave little room for error and are difficult for others to achieve. For example, perhaps you believe that unless people apologize a certain way, you can't forgive them. Perfectionism might be useful in completing work projects, but it can be damaging in relationships. Developing rigid expectations can create a life of disappointments. Holding rigid expectations can make forgiveness and reconciliation difficult.

Competition or the sense of needing to be "right" often creates a rigid pattern of communication between intimate partners. This is common when two parties do not agree on who is responsible for harm or when shared faults are not acknowledged. In many intimate conflicts, each person bears some responsibility; each one might have avoided a hurtful comment or made an apology before the quarrel became personally hurtful. The longer this pattern persists and the more hurtful the language becomes, the more difficult it is for either partner to back down. This cycle of stubbornness in acknowledging mutual fault runs counter to maintaining a healthy relationship. Either partner can choose to break out of it by offering the first apology, but if neither does, the conflict will escalate.

Living with grace involves expanding your expectation square to be more accepting of others:

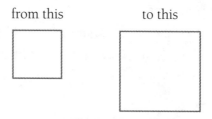

from this                    to this

Others don't have to be perfect to be okay, and neither do you. People can disappoint you at times but you can still accept and love them. To readjust your expectation square for both yourself and others, you might ask yourself these questions:

- Could this be different and still be okay?
- Can I allow myself to make a mistake and still be okay?
- Can I have a relationship that is less than perfect and still be satisfied?
- Can I allow myself to say the wrong thing once in a while and recover?

If the answer is no to any of these questions, then you may still be holding on to painful emotional memories. You may be setting up your friends and companions—who are less than perfect—to disappoint you. Rather than give up because you've made mistakes, widen your expectation square to heal and rebuild. Step away from all-or-nothing thinking and explore the myriad possibilities in between.

# Difficult People and Their Unique Circumstances

A great deal of the discussion in this book has focused on how to improve relationships by forgiving as well as reconciling with those you have harmed or those who have harmed you. For some of us, an apology may provide the bridge to renewed relationship. For others, only time and diminished emotions can heal what was broken.

However, there is a category of people who are difficult to figure out. We dub them "difficult people." They don't play by the same rules as other people you relate to. Despite your best efforts, in their presence you can feel unsure, anxious, and guilty. They are difficult to forgive because they continue patterns of behavior that are harmful. You can identify a difficult person in your life when you see the following kinds of behaviors:

- They often use your relationship for leverage. "Because you're such a helpful daughter, I would expect you to do this for me." "I know it's time for you to leave, but you're such a good employee, I'm confident that you will follow through on this for me."
- They manipulate people or situations to make themselves look good. If something bad happens, it's never their fault.
- They will surprise you with a request at an inopportune time and make you feel guilty for not acceding to their request. Later you ask yourself, "Why did I say yes to that request?"
- They will isolate you from support, especially if they have something demeaning to say.
- They appear unaware of what you feel or need.
- They will sometimes pressure you to do something you feel unsure about.
- Their emotions shift unpredictably. They may be friendly and concerned at one moment and angry and cold at another.
- No matter how much you do for them, it is never enough.

## A Difficult Person in Action

Stan had just arrived home from a hard day at work when his twelve-year-old daughter Vanessa pounced on him. "Dad, can I go to my friend Karen's house tonight for a slumber party? It's starting in an hour, so I need to know right away." (Surprise you with requests)

When Stan hesitated, his daughter begged, "Please let me go. I'm old enough for you to start trusting me. Other parents trust their kids with stuff like this." (Use relationship as leverage)

As he listened to her pleading, Stan couldn't help feeling uneasy. He didn't know the people she said were hosting the party and the whole thing seemed to have been arranged on awfully short notice. By this time, she was pushing harder, saying, "Come on, Dad, I have to let them know right away." (Pressure you to do something you feel unsure about)

When he asked what her mom thought, Vanessa responded, "Mom's at work, and you know we can't get hold of her there." (Isolate from support) "Please let me go! I'll clean my room and take out the trash for a whole week." When she realized this tactic wasn't getting anywhere, she switched gears. "You are so mean. You never let me do stuff." (Change moods quickly)

Before making a decision, Stan decided to make a few phone calls. He soon learned that the party was a graduation celebration for a high school boy. He also suspected there wouldn't be many adults present. As he kindly but firmly refused Vanessa's request, his daughter realized her efforts had failed this time.

## Forgiving a Difficult Person

Forgiving a difficult person in your life is complicated. You may have to treat her differently than others who would provide much healthier responses. Here are a few principles that will help you deal with the difficult people in your life:

1. Slow down difficult people by asking questions, requesting clarification, and finding ways to delay doing what they're asking of you. Much of their ability to do harm stems from moving fast. Slow down their requests, accusations, and attempts to manipulate. Protect yourself.

2. Be understanding. Chances are remote that they will change, since they learned their skills for being difficult somewhere in

their past. They may require more grace than the average person. Accept that this is the way they are and that your attempts to change them may not be well received. If you do want to alter their behavior, lower your expectations and focus on incremental changes.

3. Manage yourself in the presence of difficult people. Suspend your impulse to say everything you think or to reveal everything you are feeling. Mindful behavior is critical in this case. Slow your response rate down, delay them with questions, and protect yourself from unreasonable requests. You may say things like, "I have to get back to you on that," so that you have time to evaluate whether acceding to the request will harm you.

4. Minimize rigid thinking. Because difficult people tend to "push our buttons," and emphasize that their way is the right way, you may feel insecure in their presence. When they use the word *should*, you can counter with, "Help me understand what you need." Discuss other ways they could get their need met and reduce their potential to do you harm.

5. Go emotionally deaf to destructive comments. Your own pain will make you hypersensitive to devaluing comments and criticism. Don't take what they say personally. Filter their comments to focus on what is important for you to know. Realize that something else is going on in their lives. It's usually not about you.

6. Reduce your isolation. Usually, difficult people won't say harsh things or try to manipulate you when witnesses are present. Whenever you have to deal with someone who has emotionally harmed you, try to have someone else with you.

7. Minimize the amount of time you have to spend with difficult people. These people can wear you down emotionally as you expend energy protecting yourself. Decide how much time around them you can reasonably handle without "losing it."

8. Remain positive and stay on the high road. Do not be dragged down by doubts that difficult people may create. Your positive demeanor may become a positive influence in their life.

9. Figure out the best time to deal with difficult people when you have to. If you are tired, stressed, and overwhelmed by work or family pressures, this is not a time to engage with them.

There may be no forgiveness or reconciliation with a difficult person. Their negative learned behaviors can continue to do you harm, usually when you are most vulnerable. In this case, you have to protect yourself by using mindful, intentional communication.

## Overcoming Your History

Your ability to forgive and be forgiven depends on many factors, some of which you learned in childhood; others you developed in relationships along the way. While certain factors are built deeply into your core personality, others don't bother you until you interact with people who trigger old feelings. A survey participant told us that whenever he went to his childhood home to visit his parents, he felt like a child again, burdened by all his old insecurities. When he doesn't get along with his wife, her words usually call to mind these same insecurities. In many cases, these kinds of old feelings and beliefs persist; if you don't learn to manage them, they will continue to cause problems for you. To do this, practice giving yourself new messages, such as:

> Forgiveness is the accomplishment of mastery over a wound. It is the process through which an injured person first fights off, then embraces, then conquers a situation that has nearly destroyed him.
>
> —Beverly Flanigan

- This is a different situation. I can manage this.
- I may have felt that way once, but I choose to feel differently now.
- When my old emotions are triggered, I can breathe deeply, slow down, and let them pass.
- I forgive myself for areas of my life where I feel inadequate and I forgive others for contributing to this feeling.

A central theme of this chapter is that you do not have to be trapped by your past. You can practice new ways of behavior that will serve as small steps to healing your past and improving your current relationships. Some of this relies on self-talk as we described above. It also involves surrounding yourself with people who treat you with grace and acceptance, giving you room to grow.

## Questions

1. How well do you manage your emotions when you have to meet with someone you have had difficulty forgiving?

2. When you have harmed someone by something you've said or done, what steps do you take to repair the relationship?

3. What was your family drama? What evidence of it do you see in your adult life?

4. When you know you are in the presence of a difficult person, what do you do to protect yourself from potential harm?

5. Where in life could you expand your expectation square and reduce some of the stress in your life?

# CHAPTER 11

# HELPING OTHERS FORGIVE

## SERVING AS A PEACEMAKER IN THE WORLD AROUND YOU

> The thing to do is to prepare yourself so you can
> be a rainbow in somebody else's cloud.
>
> —Maya Angelou

Life experiences, family life, and career give you many opportunities to see the long-term damage created by people who were unwilling to forgive or who resisted reconciliation. On a regular basis, many professionals, such as counselors, teachers, and department managers, deal with conflicts that may require forgiveness. In our own work of helping clients resolve organizational conflict, we have found that the inability to forgive frequently keeps people stuck in uncooperative situations. This chapter explores tactics and ideas for promoting forgiveness and reconciliation when you are not directly involved in either perpetrating or experiencing harm.

As we begin to explore how to facilitate forgiveness, we offer a word of caution. People who are victims of serious offenses, such as assault, murder, incest, and abuse, may be resistant to third-party intervention because they see these acts as impossible to forgive. If one of the parties regards the marital contract as sacred, even divorce may be regarded as unforgivable. In some cases, such as those involving people who have been victims of violence, a discussion of forgiveness might not be appropriate. Broaching the subject of forgiveness without first building up another's self-respect or encouraging the healthy expression of anger may only reinforce unhealthy responses. Clergy or therapists might better address people grappling with these kinds of issues.

## We Are All Capable of Fostering Forgiveness

Most of us don't think of ourselves as facilitators of forgiveness in the lives of others. But whenever you help a family member get over a past harm, provide support for a coworker who struggles with the boss, or help a friend rebuild her marital relationship, you are facilitating forgiveness. In our study, 40 percent of the subjects had received assistance in achieving forgiveness from an outside party. Though many of those outsiders were counselors

> We have to take responsibility for what's going on in our world. We have to forgive in order to make progress. Otherwise, we're just going around in circles.
>
> —GARRISON KEILLOR

and pastors, third-party help can come from anywhere. Parents may offer to help grown children or grandchildren forgive each other. A homeowner can promote forgiveness between neighbors who have stopped speaking to each other. Counselors often help their clients figure out how to forgive people who have harmed them at some time in the past. We each live in environments in which we can serve as peacemakers, quietly promoting peace and forgiveness among those around us.

At age eighteen, Amy became part of the first coed class at a small Catholic university in the Midwest. Unfortunately, there was an eighteen-year-old boy named Brad in her class who harassed her. He constantly made fun of her, repeatedly asked her to sleep with him, and embarrassed her in public. Then one day, during a school hockey game, a hockey puck hit Brad on the side of the head. He was flown by helicopter to a hospital where he immediately underwent surgery. While the onlookers rallied and said they hoped Brad would be okay, Amy thought, "My life would be so much easier if he just died." During her first year of college, Brad had become her tormentor and bully.

A few days later, Amy felt so bad about her wish that she went to see the university priest. She confessed that she hoped Brad would die. The priest stopped the conversation abruptly and said, "Come with me, now." Without telling her where they were going, he drove her to the hospital.

The priest escorted Amy to Brad's room without saying a word. As she walked through the doors to Brad's room, she saw him in the hospital bed. He was hooked up to all kinds of monitors, and his head was swollen so much he was nearly unrecognizable. Brad's eyes were almost swollen shut, but when Amy walked to the side of the bed, he looked as if he had some recognition that she was there. Amy had not had a chance to think about what to say, so she just blurted out, "I forgive you for what you've done to me." Then she left. Brad eventually recovered from his head injury and was back at school before the year ended. But something had changed. The two never discussed the exchange in the hospital but Brad never bothered her again.

> "Come now, let us reason together," says the LORD. "Though your sins are like scarlet, they shall be as white as snow; though they are red as crimson, they shall be like wool.
>
> —ISAIAH 1:18

At their class's twenty-year reunion, Brad approached Amy. He said to her, "I hope that you can forgive me for all those mean things I did to you in college. I was part of a group of guys who had a points system for getting girls to sleep with them. You had the highest number of points attached to your name, so that's why I approached you so aggressively. I'm so sorry." The loop of forgiveness was complete. First, Amy forgave Brad and years later Brad asked for forgiveness on his own. Although it was twenty years later, the event that was initiated by a priest brought about reconciliation.

Research shows that most family members, department managers, clergy, and counselors can help people like Amy free themselves from unhealthy emotions through forgiveness. At Stanford University, research studies revealed that people who found it difficult to forgive were often able to achieve forgiveness with the help of a third party.[1]

Some of the strategies that third parties can use to help facilitate forgiveness include the following:

- Exploring spiritual beliefs can provide assurance that help is available from a higher power in working through issues requiring forgiveness.
- Discussing a past harm in the context of forgiveness can diminish the emotional impacts of the harm.

- Separating forgiveness from a need for justice can promote forgiveness without the need for revenge.
- Positive self-talk can enable someone to face difficult issues with greater confidence.
- Developing and discussing coping strategies can aid in letting go of negative emotions.
- In a supportive environment, talking about the harms a person experienced may alleviate symptoms like sadness and anger.

## Finding the Appropriate Beginning

If you suggest that a person seek forgiveness before she is ready, you will probably encounter resistance. A softer approach might be in order. For example, invite her to be open to the possibility of forgiveness as a way to heal the relationship. This invitation does not involve pressure or coercion; it only invites the person to adopt a new state of mind about the issues. You can encourage small overtures, like this: "I know you stopped speaking to your uncle several years ago. But has enough time passed? Is it time to patch up this relationship that once meant so much to you? Are there any other ways to approach the issues that bothered you?"

## Transforming Reaction to the Harm

Sometimes problems can be framed in such a way that they appear insolvable. People who have experienced harm often make statements like these: "He meant to do that to me," "She wants to make me look bad," or "He wants to see me fail." These statements frame people as adversaries with no hope of change. As a third-party helper, you can guide someone who has experienced harm by transforming her perceptions of people and the problem. Statements that might help reframe issues include the following:

- Could there be any other way to understand what happened?
- Do you think there's any possibility that the offender feels remorse for what he did?
- Is there any chance that the offender was trying to do something different than you remember?
- Share with me a memory you have about a time when this person was kind.

If the offender intended to do harm, further dialogue of this type will serve no purpose. However, if there is a slight chance that his words may have been misinterpreted or he was unaware of the harm he committed, then even small changes in perception might create the possibility of forgiveness.

You can encourage people to widen their set of expectations about the offender and the actions she committed. You can ask if the offended person can accept weakness or frailty in the offender. If not, then the opportunity for forgiveness may require more time for healing. Some researchers have found that, regardless of the approach, the amount of time dedicated to forgiveness intervention may be the most important factor. As a third party, you can encourage the harmed person to work through

> Forgiveness is not an occasional act, it is a permanent attitude.
>
> —MARTIN LUTHER KING JR.

his emotions and give healing plenty of time. During this process, you can encourage, validate, and be supportive, all of which may help as much as professional counseling.

## Promoting Reflection

Another tactic that helps promote understanding is to encourage reflection by the harmed party. You might ask, "Have you ever said or done something that has harmed another? How would you have liked that issue resolved?" Some people find that writing down the emotions associated with a harm they've perpetrated is useful. A common way to do this is to write a letter that is never mailed. Others find that journaling helps them track progress in working through their emotions. When we counseled high school students, we would often sit around a campfire. The young people were given pieces of paper and were asked to write down issues for which they needed forgiveness or for which they needed to forgive others. Then we asked them to throw their pieces of paper into the fire, symbolic of a release of the negative emotion and achieving a sense of freedom. The teens may not achieve forgiveness in this one small symbolic step, but it may give them courage to look at themselves and others differently and perhaps begin a conversation with someone that moves them farther along on their journey to forgiveness.

Another discussion that might be useful is a cost-benefit analysis. When the transgressor is a family member, the long-term grudge can expand to others in the family, thus compounding the suffering. At a job, trying to work around a colleague who has done harm may become emotionally draining and unproductive. Yet many times, the long-term benefits of repairing a broken relationship outweigh the short-term costs of initiating a discussion about the harm committed.

If the harmed person is spiritually inclined, you might encourage him to give the problem to God. The harmed person can ask God to release him from the negative emotions as well make changes in the life of the offender.

The following set of questions might be useful in helping someone work toward a sense of peace:

1. What led up to the problem we're looking at now?
2. What effect have the actions of this person had on you?
3. What's the cost of not doing anything about this issue?
4. How important is it for you to get past this issue?
5. How would you like to see your relationship change?
6. What would it take for you to forgive this person?
7. Are you willing to let go of this issue if the person apologizes or changes his behavior toward you?
8. Have you ever said something or done something to another for which you've needed forgiveness?
9. Are you aware of anything you might have done to contribute to the offender's behavior?

## Dispelling Unhelpful Beliefs

Some people may resent having to consider extending forgiveness because they view forgiveness as condoning a harmful action. They do not want to "forget" what has happened and withholding forgiveness helps them remember. Some people believe that they hold more power by withholding forgiveness. You can help counter these beliefs by clarifying the meaning and limitations of forgiveness. Here are some of the elements that should be included in this discussion:

1. Forgiveness need not mean forgetting and certainly does not mean letting down your guard so that the harm can happen again.
2. Forgiveness does not necessarily mean reconciliation.

3. Forgiveness does not mean that the offender won't be held accountable for the actions she committed.

4. Forgiveness involves letting go of negative emotions without giving up appropriate boundaries. Professor Nathaniel Wade characterizes forgiveness as "... a process in which those who have been hurt replace hostile, unforgiving feelings with more positive emotions toward the offending person without giving up appropriate physical and emotional boundaries that provide safety from hurtful people."[2]

## Changing the Conversation

Oftentimes, people delay apologizing because the negative tenor of the conversation makes them feel worse, not better. In this case, you as the third-party helper might change the direction of these conversations by encouraging the person who was harmed to take a different approach.

- Begin by talking about issues far removed from the issue of harm. Build rapport before taking on the difficult topics. Give yourself time to get ready for a focused discussion.
- Suspend criticism for a time. Take time out to stop the blame and fault-finding.
- Give the offender a way to save face. You might make comments like these: "I know that you didn't mean to hurt me when ..." or "You may have been unaware of the problem you caused ..." Giving another person a way out resets the conversation and the relationship to neutral. If the offender meant to do you harm, he will often clarify that quickly and your course of action will be clearer.

| Needs of the Person Harmed | Helper Response |
| --- | --- |
| Heal from emotional harm | Create a safe presence |
| Unsure about what forgiveness may involve | Educate the harmed person as to what forgiveness is and is not |
| Manage unpleasant memories associated with the harm | Reframe perceptions of the problem or the one who caused the harm |
| Reduce negative emotions | Invite forgiveness |

# When You Are Helping the Offender

In the initial phase of helping an offender, gather information about the situation that occurred by asking, "From your perspective, tell me what happened." If you uncover any misunderstanding or miscommunication, you might be able to defuse the issue quickly. However, if the offender did have malicious intent, you may ask the victim, "Tell me how you might act differently next time?" or "Would you like to do something to repair the relationship?" Just as you invite the person who was harmed to consider offering forgiveness, you encourage the one who has committed the harm to seek forgiveness.

You can encourage an offender to make an apology as well as discussing an appropriate way to deliver that apology, such as a letter, a phone call, face-to-face interaction, or words conveyed by a mediator. You might even role-play a potential conversation to practice possible responses to tough issues. We have found this last tactic especially useful in helping people prepare for seeking forgiveness or reconciliation.

The following set of questions might help someone think about a harm he committed, why seeking forgiveness is necessary, and how the relationship might be repaired:

1. Are you okay with this relationship the way it is now?

2. Are you interested in restoring the relationship to how it used to be?

3. Are you interested in taking responsibility for your part in the stresses in this relationship?

4. Does it matter to you if the other person is hurting or sad?

5. Can you understand why the other person might be offended?

6. Is there anything you wish you had done differently in this situation?

7. Are you willing to make this situation right?

8. Are you open to offering an apology to clear the air?

9. Do you feel any regret, guilt, or remorse over anything you have done in this conflict?

10. What can you do to signal positive intentions toward the person you have harmed?

## Acknowledge the Wrongdoing

There are several steps you can take to coach an offender toward offering an acceptable apology. But before that can happen, she must acknowledge her wrongdoing. For example, one of our mediation cases involved Dina, a woman whose work required extensive travel. During our discussion, Dina responded to her husband's initial complaint by offering explanations and excuses: "On that Asian trip, I was jet-lagged and lonesome. I had too much to drink and spent the night with an associate. It didn't mean anything really. We both felt stupid the next morning." Her statement reveals some facts but doesn't meet the test of an effective apology. She seems to be dodging responsibility.

For an apology to be accepted, the party who seeks forgiveness must take responsibility for the harm committed. In Dina's case, she needs to recognize that her defensiveness probably won't help her spouse to forgive her. A simple, unencumbered acknowledgment of loss or hurt would probably be more effective. An admission that "I made a mistake and I take full responsibility for that" is more likely to lead to forgiveness.

## Facilitate Indirect Apologies

In our experience as organizational consultants, it is not unusual for an offender, especially one of higher status, to meet the offended person only partway. In one of our cases, a department head presented information at a team meeting that was based on an employee's research. The department head gave the impression that he had done the research himself. After being confronted about this, the department head said he was willing to apologize to the employee privately but not admit guilt in front of his team.

At this point, consultants or helpers still have a role to play. You can bring clarity to both sides about what is negotiable and what is not. You may point out the risk of losing the good work done thus far because of a nonnegotiable demand. Sometimes, you will help each party move toward forgiveness, while recognizing that, in the workplace, it may be difficult to achieve total satisfaction.

Similar patterns emerge with people who accept responsibility but cannot or will not utter the words *I'm sorry*. These individuals may not be willing to amend their offending behaviors, make restitution, or do either. In these cases, you might encourage an indirect apology.

Indirect apologies are common in organizations where there is a strict hierarchy and it would be unusual for managers to apologize directly to their subordinates. For instance, a doctor may agree to stop criticizing hospital staff in front of others, but will not apologize for her past behavior. Whether or not this results in forgiveness depends entirely on the staff members' perspectives. Sometimes, an indirect strategy will work fine for certain individuals or be appropriate for specific contexts.

As discussed earlier, an effective apology includes elements such as acknowledgment of wrongdoing, acceptance of responsibility, development of empathy toward the other, and a promise not to repeat the harm. Restitution may or may not be needed, and, if necessary, it may have to be negotiated. There are various kinds of effective apologies. They may not be spoken in so many words or they may be conditional. In our work, we have found this to be especially true in hierarchical organizational settings.

## Promise to Cease the Offending Behavior

Forgiveness is supported by agreements that call for new behavior and invoke sanctions if offenses are repeated. In coaching someone who intends to change his behavior, try to encourage him to use language like this: "This will never happen again. I promise." If the other person does not believe this promise, no polishing of the apology will lead to forgiveness. The offended person also needs to agree to accept the consequences if he breaks his promise. Asking forgiveness repeatedly for the same offense is not acceptable.

| NEEDS OF THE OFFENDER | HELPER RESPONSE |
|---|---|
| Rebuild moral reputation | Invite her to make an apology |
| End offending behavior | Create boundaries |
| Express remorse | Nonjudgmental listening |
| Desire for reconciliation | Recognize offender's loss |
| Embarrassed to admit wrongdoing | Invite act of restitution |

Whatever the circumstances of your life, you have the ability to make positive, lasting contributions to those around you. As a sensitive and compassionate listener, you provide an opportunity for people who have been hurt to express their pain. You can empathize and provide support. As a helper, you can encourage others to find ways to deal with the harm they experienced. In some cases, you can help them think about what they might say to the person who has done them harm as well as how to heal, how to move on, and how to get over it.

You can encourage people who have caused harm to accept responsibility for their actions, express remorse, make amends for what they've done, and, where possible, apologize for their harmful actions. In helping people repair what they've broken, you serve as a peacemaker.

## Questions

1. Have you ever helped another person offer or seek forgiveness? If so, what was the experience like for you?

2. What has helping others navigate the process of forgiveness taught you about your own ability (or inability) to forgive?

3. Would you ever say no to a request for help from someone who wanted to forgive or be forgiven? If so, what would be your reasoning?

4. If you do say no to a request for help, what resources might you suggest to assist your friends, family members, or colleagues?

# CONCLUDING THOUGHTS ─────────

As we look back at the insights from this book, we find that forgiving a deep harm is neither simple nor easy. Human nature simultaneously includes a desire to forgive and a need for revenge. You must decide which side of your nature to encourage and which to ignore. The degree of harm suffered and your relationship to the person who harmed you will both factor into that decision. For example, did the offender offer an apology and did you find it adequate? Do you feel need for reconciliation and do you want to pursue it? At a less transparent level, even the values of your community influence how you react to harm, often without your even realizing it.

Forgiveness involves several perspectives—psychological (you work out issues within yourself), relational (you work out issues with others), and spiritual (you work out issues with God or whatever sources your spirit draws sustenance from). The perspective you choose depends on the kind of issue you're dealing with. If you are worried about working through old emotions and annoying memories, you will be more interested in psychological healing. If you've had harsh words with someone important in your life and resentment lingers, you may need to initiate a discussion to repair the harm. If you believe that your failures are creating doubts about the health of your spiritual life, you may turn to spiritual healing. Whichever perspective you choose, you need to identify a path and a journey that heals the wounds you carry within you.

In this book, we have spoken of forgiveness as a gift to yourself and to others. A gift is something we give freely with grace and appreciation. We encourage you to receive the gift of forgiveness and share it with those around you. Perhaps it is time to grant someone a pardon for old offenses.

Perhaps it is time to forgive yourself for a failure that you regretted and attempted to repair. It's time to move on with life, let go, and develop new stories for your journey.

We want to close with a few of the important insights in each of the three dimensions of life that we've shared along the way:

## Psychological

- Forgiveness is possible even in the most harmful of situations. We heard amazing words from Holocaust survivors, the parents of Columbine students, and individuals who've overcome the emotional damage wreaked by sexual assault and abuse. The consistent message is this: it can be done.

- People who give and receive forgiveness experience many benefits. Some of these are physical, such as relief from back pain or lower blood pressure. But other benefits include freedom from annoying doubts and memories, and repair to relationships that once were important to them.

- Forgiveness rarely just happens. It generally requires intentional choices and renewed ways of thinking. Your mind creates neural pathways that remember harm, but these pathways can be changed though self-talk, meditation, and friends who support you.

- Forgiveness does not mean forgetting. In fact, in cases of abuse or crime, forgetting may not be appropriate. Your memories provide an important tool for protecting yourself from similar harm. But forgiveness may mean letting go of the need to relive the past over and over again. When you are able to forgive, negative thoughts diminish over time.

## Relational

- Forgiveness is a process and a journey and it may be different for each of us. Some people may require a spoken apology and others may be satisfied with a change of behavior. For some, saying *I'm sorry* may only be the first step in a journey of reconciliation. What's most important is to keep moving forward on your journey and toward the healing you deserve.

- The ability to forgive others may be linked to the ability to forgive yourself. The two processes are often connected. Forgiving yourself can improve relationships with others and forgiving others can help you feel better about yourself.

- If you have offended another, an apology may be the most important action you can take to build a bridge and repair the relationship. An apology demonstrates commitment to the relationship and caring for the other person.

- If you choose to apologize, incorporate the best elements of an effective apology. These include acknowledging the offense, accepting responsibility for your contribution to the offense, expressing remorse for your actions, making a commitment not to repeat similar behavior, and offering reparations to repair the damage you've caused. At the same time, be gracious in accepting apologies from others.

## Spiritual

- Forgiveness enables your spirit to become right once more with God or with sacred sources in your life, one of the most important relationships that many of us have. It provides a fresh beginning in life's journey.

- We each possess the capacity to be peacemakers in this world, and forgiveness provides a way we can influence the lives and relationships around us. Holding grudges or seeking revenge only escalate emotional damage in our families and communities. Let your motto be something similar to the words of the old folk song, "Let there be peace on earth and let it begin with me."

- Be someone who contributes to the healing of others. Use your skills of listening, inviting, and encouraging to facilitate forgiveness in those around you. Surround yourself with a circle of peace and forgiveness.

Many well-known leaders speak of forgiveness and its power of healing in the following statements made during their lives:

"Having looked the past in the eye, having asked for forgiveness and having made amends, let us shut the door on the past—not in order to forget it, but in order not to allow it to imprison us."

Desmond Tutu, South African Anglican Bishop

"Give the world the best you have and it may never be enough. Give your best anyway. For you see, in the end, it is between you and God. It was never between you and them anyway."

Mother Teresa

"We cannot change the past, but we can change our attitude toward it. Uproot guilt and plant forgiveness. Tear out arrogance and seed humility. Exchange love for hate ... making the present comfortable and the future promising."

Maya Angelou

Forgiveness is a choice. It is granting yourself and others freedom to make mistakes and to begin again. We, the authors, consider ourselves practitioners of peace and we invite you to join us in building a healthier world through the gift of forgiveness.

# ACKNOWLEDGMENTS ———

The authors wish to thank the many graduate students whose interests in the topic of forgiveness energized and informed our work. Some past graduates have followed this writing closely and contributed feedback, particularly Joe Cassa, Rob Jones, Carisa Scott, and Dawn Watson. As well as editorial suggestions, Devin Rau assisted with collating and coding the survey research.

We invited many colleagues to read chapters that pertained to their fields: Frank Dance, John and Martie Fiske, David Fulton, Ned Heppenstall, Jim Laurie, Elizabeth Loescher, Alice Mack, Scott Poland, Nancy Simon Purdon, Ed and Renata Selig, and Carol Zak-Dance. The background and writing experience of these readers added immeasurably to the project. This is a more tightly focused book thanks to their input.

We took advantage of recently retired friends who understood the material from the perspective of general readers. Laura Finn, Ron Gager, Suzanne Greene, Rick and Susie Grossman, Nancy Karklins, Phyllis Beck Katz, Lynn Skall, and Pat Spitzmiller gave us invaluable feedback. They corrected our grammar, suggested more suitable phrases, and occasionally challenged our theology. Their time and attention to detail are much appreciated.

Gratitude goes to the consistent guidance of Emily Wichland, our editor at SkyLight Paths Publishing. Emily was insightful from the beginning of our association, patient as we balanced this work with major life changes, and encouraging throughout the process. She coordinated an able team of artists, publicists, and copy editors who advanced the book in areas outside our competencies. Despite two thousand miles of separation, Emily capably captured the purpose and spirit of our endeavor.

# NOTES

## Chapter 1: The Nature of Forgiveness

1. Fred Luskin, *Forgive for Good: A Power Prescription for Health and Happiness* (San Francisco: HarperOne, 2003), 19.
2. Jack Kornfield, *After the Ecstasy, the Laundry: How the Heart Grows Wise on the Spiritual Path* (New York: Bantam, 2001).
3. Everett Worthington, *Forgiving and Reconciling: Bridges to Wholeness and Hope* (Downers Grove, IL.: InterVarsity Press, 2003).
4. Saima Noreen, Raynette Bierman, and Malcolm Macleod, "Forgiving You Is Hard, but Forgetting Seems Easy: Can Forgiveness Facilitate Forgetting?" *Psychological Science* 257, no. 7 (2014): 1295–1302.
5. Pope Benedict XVI, *Time Magazine* (June 7, 2010); http://content.time.com/time/magazine/article/0,9171,1992408,00.html (accessed April 25, 2014).
6. Dennis Linn, Sheila Linn, and Matthew Linn, *Don't Forgive Too Soon: Extending the Two Hands That Heal* (Mahwah, NJ: Paulist Press, 1997).

## Chapter 2: Ways We Experience Forgiveness

1. Laura Davis, *I Thought We'd Never Speak Again: The Road from Estrangement to Reconciliation* (New York: Quill, 2002), 313–314.
2. Pema Chödrön, *The Places That Scare You: A Guide to Fearlessness in Difficult Times* (Boston: Shambhala, 2001), 50.
3. Susyn Reeve and Sheri Rosenthal, "The Power of Forgiveness in Action," www.thepowerofforgiveness.com/pdf/Forgiveness_in_Action.pdf (accessed August 15, 2014).
4. Robert Enright, *The Forgiving Life: A Pathway to Overcoming Resentment and Creating a Legacy of Love* (Washington, DC: American Psychological Association, 2012), 70.
5. See https://showyou.com/therealmischief/y-_7T7QQ90Jtk/ame-emanuel-church-full-sermon-emanuel-ame-church-holds (accessed June 23, 2015).
6. "Victim's daughter to church shooter: 'I forgive you,'" CNN.com, June 19, 2015; www.cnn.com/videos/us2015/06/19/families-of-charleston-church-shooting-address-killer-orig.com (accessed June 23, 2015).

7. See www.nytimes.com/aponline/2015/06/19/us/ap-us-charleston-shooting-the-latest.html (accessed June 23, 2015), 1.

8. Josh Levs and Azadeh Ansari, "Photos Show Victim's Mother Forgives Killer, Halts Hanging in Time," CNN News, www.cnn.com/2014/04/17/world/meast/iran-execution-photos-mother-forgives/index.html (accessed June 8, 2015).

9. Henry Charles, *Forgiveness Considered* (Bloomington, IN: Xlibris Corp, 2011), 5.

## Chapter 3: Benefits of Forgiving and Being Forgiven

1. Robert Enright, *Forgiveness Is a Choice: A Step-by-Step Process for Resolving Anger and Restoring Hope* (Washington, DC: American Psychological Association, 2001), 256–258.

2. J. Carson, *Duke Study Links Forgiveness to Less Back Pain, Depression* (Durham, NC: Duke University Medical Center, 2003).

3. Redford Williams and Virginia Williams, *Anger Kills: Seventeen Strategies for Controlling the Hostility That Can Harm Your Health* (New York: Random House, 1993).

4. John F. Kennedy, Speech at Loyola College Alumni Banquet, Baltimore, Maryland, February 18, 1958, "Loyola College Alumni Banquet, Baltimore, Maryland, 18 February 1958" folder, Senate Files, box 899, John F. Kennedy Presidential Library.

5. Carol Watson and L. Richard Hoffman, "Managers as Negotiators," *Leadership Quarterly* 7 (1) 1996.

6. Charles Griswold, "On Forgiveness," *New York Times,* December 26, 2010, F1.

7. Frans deWaal, *Peacemaking Among Primates* (Cambridge, MA: Harvard University Press, 1989), 237–249.

8. Michael McCullough, "The Forgiveness Instinct," *Greater Good: The Science of a Meaningful Life* (March 1, 2008): 2.

## Chapter 4: Resisting the Practice of Forgiveness

1. Robert Karen, *The Forgiving Self* (New York: Anchor Books, 2001), 14.

2. Michael McCullough, "The Forgiveness Instinct," *Greater Good: The Science of a Meaningful Life* (March 1, 2008): 2.

3. Sidney Simon and Suzanne Simon, *Forgiveness: How to Make Peace with Your Past and Get On with Your Life* (New York: Grand Central, 1990), 85.

4. Tom Mauser, *Walking in Daniel's Shoes* (Point Pleasant Beach, NJ: Ocean Star, 2012), 295–300.

5. Robert Karen, *The Forgiving Self* (New York: Anchor Books, 2001), 14.

6. Jared Diamond, "Vengeance Is Ours," *The New Yorker,* April 7, 2008, 74–87.

7. Francis Bacon, "On Revenge," http://en.wikiquote.org/wiki/Francis_Bacon (accessed May 15, 2014).

8. William Tidwell, *Conflict Resolved? A Critical Assessment of Conflict Resolution* (London: Pinter, 1998), 135–136.

9. Simon Wiesenthal, *The Sunflower: The Possibilities and Limits of Forgiveness* (New York: Schocken Books, 1998).

10. "Museum of Conflict," *The Smithsonian Magazine*, January 2014, 92.

## Chapter 5: What Facilitates Forgiveness?

1. Donald Walker and Richard Gorsuch, "Forgiveness within the Big Five Personality Model," *Personality and Individual Differences* 32 (2002): 1127–1137.

2. See W. Carroll, www.forgiving.org/conference archive/conference_1. htm#ellis (accessed April 12, 2012), and G. Veenstra, "Psychological Concepts of Forgiveness," *Journal of Psychology and Christianity* 11 (1992): 160–169 for studies linking religion and forgiveness.

3. Stephen Poos-Benson, *Sent to Soar: Fulfill Your Divine Potential for Yourself and for the World* (Wheaton, IL.: Quest Books, 2014), 204.

4. Robert Karen, *The Forgiving Self* (New York: Anchor Books, 2001), 162.

5. Michelle Girard and Etienne Mullet, "Propensity to Forgive in Adolescents, Young Adults, Older Adults, and Elderly People," *Journal of Adult Development* 4 (1997): 209–220.

6. Jose Orathinkle, Alfons Vansteenwegen, and Roger Burggraeve, "Are Demographics Important for Forgiveness?" *Family Journal* (2008): 16–20.

7. Karl Acquino, Thomas M. Tripp, and Robert J. Bies, "Getting Even or Moving On? Procedural Justice and Types of Offense as Predictors of Revenge, Forgiveness, Reconciliation, and Avoidance in Organizations," *Journal of Applied Psychology* 91, no. 3 (2006): 654.

8. Lord George Herbert, http://en.wikiquote.org/wiki/Forgiveness (accessed June 15, 2014).

9. Aaron Lazare, "Apology in Medical Practice," *JAMA* 296, no. 11 (2006): 1401–1404.

10. Scott Atran and Jeremy Ginges, "How Words Could End a War," www.nytimes.com/2009/01/25/opinion/25atran.html (accessed August 15, 2014).

11. Ibid.

12. Rajeev Bhargava, "Restoring Decency to Barbaric Societies" in eds. Robert Rotberg and Dennis Thompson, *Truth and Justice* (Princeton, NJ: Princeton University Press, 2000).

13. Jean-Marie Kamatali, "Following Orders in Rwanda," *New York Times,* April 5, 2014, A19.

## Chapter 6: The Path to Forgiveness

1. Martin Luther King Jr., www.quotes-inspirational.com/quotes/forgiveness/ html (accessed May 25, 2015).
2. David Brooks, "The Act of Vigorous Forgiving," www.nytimes. com/2015/02/10/opinion/david-brooks-the-act-of-rigorous-forgiving.html?rr ef=collection%2Fcolumn%2Fdavid-brooks (accessed April 25, 2014).
3. Dennis, Sheila, and Matthew Linn, *Don't Forgive Too Soon: Extending the Two Hands That Heal* (Mahwah, NJ: Paulist Press, 1997), 29.
4. Ibid, 30.
5. Douglas Kelley and Vincent Waldron, "An Investigation of Forgiveness-Seeking Communication and Relational Outcomes," *Communication Quarterly* 53, no. 3 (2005): 339–358.
6. "Talking It Out: Getting to Agreement," zinnmediation.com (accessed September 12, 2014).
7. Fred Luskin, *Forgive for Good: A Proven Prescription for Health and Happiness* (San Francisco: HarperOne, 2003).
8. Everett Worthington, *Forgiving and Reconciling* (Downers Grove, IL.: InterVarsity Press, 2003), 183.

## Chapter 7: Self-Forgiveness

1. www.nytimes.com/1998/09/16/opinion/forgiving-george-wallace.html.
2. Ibid.
3. Lewis Smedes, *Forgive to Forget: Healing the Hurts We Don't Deserve* (New York: HarperOne, 2007), 96.
4. Richard Hanson, www.wildmind.org/blogs/on-practice/the-art-of-self-forgiveness (accessed February 24, 2015).
5. Sidney Simon and Suzanne Simon, *Forgiveness: How to Make Peace with Your Past and Get On with Your Life* (New York: Grand Central, 1990), 119.
6. Smedes, *Forgive to Forget*, 104.

## Chapter 8: The Role of Apology

1. Kathryn Schultz, "On Being Wrong," www.ted.com/talks/kathryn_schulz_ on_being_wrong (accessed March 11, 2014).
2. Karina Schumann, "Does Love Mean Never Having to Say You're Sorry?" *Journal of Social and Personal Relationships* 29, no. 7 (2002): 997–1010.
3. David Brooks, "The Act of Rigorous Forgiving," *New York Times*, February 10, 2015, A21.
4. Aaron Lazare, *On Apology* (New York: Oxford University Press, 2005).
5. "Bombing of Tokyo Marked by Mondale," *New York Times*, March 11, 1995, D1.

6. Hillary Clinton, "U.S. Apologizes for Syphilis Tests in Guatemala," *New York Times*, October 1, 2010, A3.

7. Arnold Schwarzenegger, "Sexual Harassment, Herman Cain and the Terminator," *Star Tribune*, November 8, 2011, A4.

8. "Packard Offers Apology Without Saying for What," *New York Times*, August 26, 1995, A2.

9. Tiger Woods, televised news conference, Ponte Beach, Florida, February 20, 2010.

## Chapter 9: Reconciliation

1. Everett Worthington, *Forgiving and Reconciling* (Downers Grove, IL: InterVarsity Press, 2003), 17–19.

2. Robert Enright, *The Forgiving Life: A Pathway to Overcoming Resentment and Creating a Legacy of Love* (Washington, DC: American Psychological Association, 2012).

3. Laura Davis, *I Thought We'd Never Speak Again: The Road from Estrangement to Reconciliation* (New York: Quill, 2002), 313–314.

4. Eli Finkel, Caryl Rusbult, Madoka Kumashior, and Peggy Hannon, "Dealing with Betrayal in Close Relationships: Does Commitment Promote Forgiveness?" *Journal of Personality and Social Psychology* 82, no. 6 (2002): 956–974.

5. Bruce Patterson and Dan O'Hair, "Relational Reconciliation: Toward a More Comprehensive Model of Relation Development," *Communication Research Reports* 9, no. 2 (1992): 119–129.

## Chapter 10: When Forgiving and Reconciling Are Difficult

1. These five factors are based on the work of Robert Karen, *The Forgiving Self* (New York: Anchor Books, 2001).

2. Leslie Brody and Judith Hall, "Gender, Emotion and Expression," in Michael Lewis and Jeanette Haviland-Jones, eds., *Handbook of Emotions* (New York: The Guilford Press, 2000), 338–347.

3. Norman Doidge, *The Brain That Changes Itself* (New York: Penguin, 2007).

## Chapter 11: Helping Others Forgive

1. Fred Luskin, *Forgive for Good: A Proven Prescription for Health and Happiness* (New York: HarperOne, 2003).

2. Nathaniel Wade and Everett L. Worthington Jr., "In Search of a Common Core: A Content Analysis of Interventions to Promote Forgiveness," *Psychotherapy: Theory, Research, Practice, Training* 42, no. 2 (2005): 160–177.

# SUGGESTIONS FOR FURTHER LEARNING

We have listed some resources below; we have not examined, certified, or warranted the associations or the professionals listed. However, along with recommendations from trusted friends or family members, these lists of resources may be helpful to interested readers.

## Books

Davis, Laura. *I Thought We'd Never Speak Again: The Road from Estrangement to Reconciliation.* New York: Quill, 2003.

Editors at SkyLight Paths. *The Forgiveness Handbook: Spiritual Wisdom and Practice for the Journey to Freedom, Healing and Peace.* Woodstock, VT: SkyLight Paths Publishing, 2014.

Ford, Marcia. *The Sacred Art of Forgiveness: Forgiving Ourselves and Others through God's Grace.* Woodstock, VT: SkyLight Paths Publishing, 2006.

Kedar, Karyn D. *The Bridge to Forgiveness: Stories and Prayers for Finding God and Restoring Wholeness.* Woodstock, VT: Jewish Lights Publishing, 2007.

Linn, Dennis, Sheila Linn, and Matthew Linn. *Don't Forgive Too Soon: Extending the Two Hands That Heal.* Mahwah, NJ: Paulist Press, 1997.

Luskin, Fred. *Forgive for Good: A Power Prescription for Health and Happiness.* San Francisco: Harper, 2002.

Simon, Sidney, and Suzanne Simon. *Forgiveness: How to Make Peace with Your Past and Get On with Your Life.* New York: Grand Central, 1991.

Smedes, Lewis B. *The Art of Forgiving: When You Need to Forgive and Don't Know How.* New York: Ballantine Books, 1997.

Tutu, Desmond, and Mpho Tutu. *The Book of Forgiving: The Fourfold Path for Healing Ourselves and Our World.* New York: Harper One, 2015.

Wiesenthal, Simon. *The Sunflower: The Possibilities and Limits of Forgiveness.* New York: Schocken Books, 1998.

Worthington, Everett L. *Forgiving and Reconciling: Bridges to Wholeness and Hope.* Downers Grove IL: IVP, 2003.

## Websites

**aapc.org**

The American Association of Pastoral Counselors has as its mission bringing "healing, hope, and wholeness to individuals, families and communities by expanding and equipping spiritually grounded and psychologically informed care, counseling and psychotherapy."

**helpPRO.com**

This site offers blogs and a directory of mental health professionals, listed by state, city, specialty, treatment method, cost, and so on. It has search capabilities by zip code, type of insurance, and problem identified.

**helpstartshere.org**

This site offers a few online directories to help search for the right therapist. These sites list thousands of clinical social workers, psychologists, psychiatrists, and other licensed mental health professionals. The directories are helpPRO.com, networktherapy.com and psychologytoday.com.

**networktherapy.com**

This site "allows visitors to research many different mental illnesses and to conduct easy geographic searches for therapists." It also suggests looking in the phone book under "social service organizations" and "mental health." The majority of the support groups listed address physical and mental health issues (eating disorders, alcoholism, chronic illness).

**psychologytoday.com**

This site consists of detailed professional listings for psychologists, psychiatrists, therapists, counselors, group therapy, and treatment centers in the United States and Canada. Of the sites listed here, this seems to be the simplest one to navigate. The home page allows the user to search by price, gender, or alphabetically by name. You can also view profiles, phone numbers, and email addresses of professionals listed.

**Radicalforgiveness.com**

This site offers information about coaches who specialize in forgiveness.

# *Inspiration*

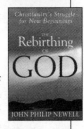

## The Rebirthing of God
Christianity's Struggle for New Beginnings
*By John Philip Newell*
Drawing on modern prophets from East and West, and using the holy island of Iona as an icon of new beginnings, Celtic poet, peacemaker and scholar John Philip Newell dares us to imagine a new birth from deep within Christianity, a fresh stirring of the Spirit.
6 x 9, 160 pp, HC, 978-1-59473-542-4 **$19.99**

## Finding God Beyond Religion: A Guide for Skeptics, Agnostics & Unorthodox Believers Inside & Outside the Church
*By Tom Stella; Foreword by The Rev. Canon Marianne Wells Borg*
Reinterprets traditional religious teachings central to the Christian faith for people who have outgrown the beliefs and devotional practices that once made sense to them.
6 x 9, 160 pp, Quality PB, 978-1-59473-485-4 **$16.99**

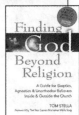

## Fully Awake and Truly Alive: Spiritual Practices to Nurture Your Soul
*By Rev. Jane E. Vennard; Foreword by Rami Shapiro*
Illustrates the joys and frustrations of spiritual practice, offers insights from various religious traditions and provides exercises and meditations to help us become more fully alive.
6 x 9, 208 pp, Quality PB, 978-1-59473-473-1 **$16.99**

## Perennial Wisdom for the Spiritually Independent
Sacred Teachings—Annotated & Explained
*Annotation by Rami Shapiro; Foreword by Richard Rohr*
Weaves sacred texts and teachings from the world's major religions into a coherent exploration of the five core questions at the heart of every religion's search.
5½ x 8½, 336 pp, Quality PB, 978-1-59473-515-8 **$16.99**

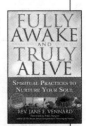

## The Sacred Art of Forgiveness:
Forgiving Ourselves and Others through God's Grace
*By Marcia Ford*
Through real-life examples, penetrating reflections, Scriptures and practical suggestions, outlines the steps that one by one can help you to forgive.
8 x 8, 176 pp, Quality PB, 978-1-59473-175-4 **$18.99**

**Journeys of Simplicity:** Traveling Light with Thomas Merton, Bashō, Edward Abbey, Annie Dillard & Others *By Philip Harnden*
5 x 7¼, 144 pp, Quality PB, 978-1-59473-181-5 **$12.99**

**Saving Civility:** 52 Ways to Tame Rude, Crude & Attitude for a Polite Planet
*By Sara Hacala* 6 x 9, 240 pp, Quality PB, 978-1-59473-314-7 **$16.99**

**Spiritually Healthy Divorce:** Navigating Disruption with Insight & Hope
*By Carolyne Call* 6 x 9, 224 pp, Quality PB, 978-1-59473-288-1 **$16.99**

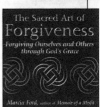

*Or phone, fax, mail or email to:* SKYLIGHT PATHS Publishing
Sunset Farm Offices, Route 4 • P.O. Box 237 • Woodstock, Vermont 05091
Tel: (802) 457-4000 • Fax: (802) 457-4004 • www.skylightpaths.com
*Credit card orders:* (800) 962-4544 (8:30AM–5:30PM EST Monday–Friday)
*Generous discounts on quantity orders. SATISFACTION GUARANTEED. Prices subject to change.*

# *Professional Spiritual & Pastoral Care Resources*

## Change & Conflict in Your Congregation (Even If You Hate Both)
How to Implement Conscious Choices, Manage Emotions & Build a
Thriving Christian Community *By Rev. Anita L. Bradshaw, PhD* Positive, relational
strategies for navigating change and channeling conflict into a stronger sense of
community. 6 x 9, 176 pp, Quality PB, 978-1-59473-578-3 **$16.99**

## Professional Spiritual & Pastoral Care
A Practical Clergy and Chaplain's Handbook
*Edited by Rabbi Stephen B. Roberts, MBA, MHL, BCJC*
An essential resource integrating the classic foundations of pastoral care with
the latest approaches to spiritual care, specifically in acute care hospitals,
behavioral health facilities, rehabilitation centers and long-term care facilities.
6 x 9, 480 pp, HC, 978-1-59473-312-3 **$50.00**

## Spiritual Guidance across Religions
A Sourcebook for Spiritual Directors & Other Professionals Providing
Counsel to People of Differing Faith Traditions
*Edited by Rev. John R. Mabry, PhD*
This comprehensive professional resource offers valuable information for pro-
viding spiritual guidance to people from a wide variety of faith traditions. Covers
the world's major faith traditions as well as interfaith, blended and independent
approaches to spirituality. 6 x 9, 400 pp, HC, 978-1-59473-546-2 **$50.00**

## College & University Chaplaincy in the 21st Century
A Multifaith Look at the Practice of Ministry on Campuses across America
*Edited by Rev. Dr. Lucy Forster-Smith; Foreword by Rev. Janet M. Cooper Nelson*
Examines the challenges of the secular context of today's college or university campus.
6 x 9, 368pp, HC, 978-1-59473-516-5 **$40.00**

## Disaster Spiritual Care
Practical Clergy Responses to Community, Regional and National Tragedy
*Edited by Rabbi Stephen B. Roberts, MBA, MHL, BCJC*
*and Rev. Willard W. C. Ashley, Sr., MDiv, DMin, DH*
The definitive guidebook for counseling not only the victims of disaster but also
the clergy and caregivers who are called to service in the wake of crisis.
6 x 9, 384 pp, HC, 978-1-59473-240-9 **$50.00**

## How to Be a Perfect Stranger, 6th Edition
The Essential Religious Etiquette Handbook
*Edited by Stuart M. Matlins and Arthur J. Magida*
The indispensable guidebook to help the well-meaning guest when visiting other
people's religious ceremonies. Covers: **African American Methodist Churches • Assemblies
of God • Bahá'í Faith • Baptist • Buddhist • Christian Church (Disciples of Christ) • Christian
Science (Church of Christ, Scientist) • Churches of Christ • Episcopalian and Anglican • Hindu
• Islam • Jehovah's Witnesses • Jewish • Lutheran • Mennonite/Amish • Methodist • Mormon
(Church of Jesus Christ of Latter-day Saints) • Native American/First Nations • Orthodox
Churches • Pentecostal Church of God • Presbyterian • Quaker (Religious Society of Friends)
• Reformed Church in America/Canada • Roman Catholic • Seventh-day Adventist • Sikh •
Unitarian Universalist • United Church of Canada • United Church of Christ**
6 x 9, 416 pp, Quality PB, 978-1-59473-593-6 **$19.99**
"The things Miss Manners forgot to tell us about religion."
—*Los Angeles Times*

**Caresharing:** A Reciprocal Approach to Caregiving and Care Receiving in the
Complexities of Aging, Illness or Disability *By Marty Richards*
6 x 9, 256 pp, Quality PB, 978-1-59473-286-7 **$16.99**; HC, 978-1-59473-247-8 **$24.99**

**Learning to Lead:** Lessons in Leadership for People of Faith
*Edited by Rev. Williard W. C. Ashley Sr., MDiv, DMin, DH*
6 x 9, 384 pp, HC, 978-1-59473-432-8 **$40.00**

## The Perfect Stranger's Guide to Funerals and Grieving Practices
A Guide to Etiquette in Other People's Religious Ceremonies
*Edited by Stuart M. Matlins* 6 x 9, 240 pp, Quality PB, 978-1-893361-20-1 **$16.95**